Scottish History

ISBN 0 - 75253 - 038 - 0 (Hardback)
ISBN 0 - 75253 - 881 - 0 (Paperback)

This is a Parragon Book
This edition published in 2000
Parragon
Queen Street House
4 Queen Street
Bath BA1 1HE ,UK

Printed in Indonesia
Produced for Parragon by
Foundry Design & Production, a part of
The Foundry Creative Media Company Ltd,
Crabtree Hall, Crabtree Lane,
Fulham, London, SW6 6TY

Grateful thanks to Josephine Cutts
and Jason Wallace

A copy of the CIP data for this book is
available from the British Library.

Scottish History

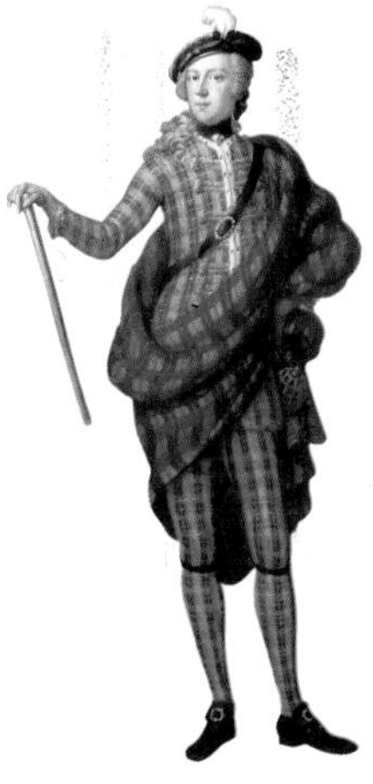

General Editor:
Dr James Mackay

Contents

Contents

Introduction

SCOTLAND can be defined precisely as that part of Britain lying to the north of England and separated from it by the natural boundaries of the Solway Firth, the Sark, Esk and Liddel, the Cheviot Hills and the Tweed, all but a short distance from its mouth where the frontier veers round the northern outskirts of Berwick. The town of Berwick was once Scotland's largest seaport and one of its four royal burghs; it was occupied by Edward I of England in 1296 but only became a part of England, irrevocably, in 1482.

Scotland also includes the Hebrides, the Orkney Islands and the Shetland Islands, and has a total area of 30,418 square miles (78,783 square km). At the census of 1991 the country had a population of 4,957,300 – not much more than the population of 60 years earlier (4,842,980) and actually rather less than the 1938 estimate of 4,993,126. However the natural increase in the birth rate has been offset by a net emigration of about a million Scots in the course of the twentieth century alone.

The fairly stable population has sometimes been regarded as evidence of the stagnation of Scotland and this, in turn, has been attributed to the fact that the Scots are a nation without a country of their own. Comparisons with other dispossessed peoples, such as the Basques and the Kurds, are often made, although Scotland is in an infinitely better position than either of these nations in that its population resides within a clearly defined area, a historic entity which (Berwick apart) has preserved its territorial boundaries. Furthermore, Scotland (at the time of writing) is on the brink of devolution, with its own

▲ *Alexander Fleming*

parliament. This has come about after a gap of almost three centuries.

It remains to be seen whether the Scots will be content with some form of autonomy or will regard devolution as a stepping stone to full sovereignty. If Slovakia is a viable country divorced from the Czech Republic, might not Scotland, the poor relation of England, also rediscover itself if it stands on its own feet? This argument is strengthened by the doctrine of subsidiarity, whereby membership of the European Community makes allowance for ethnic minorities and autonomous regions in the member countries.

Although Scotland voluntarily surrendered its sovereignty in 1707, it retained its legal system, and to this day Scots law differs in many respects from its English counterpart. The Church of Scotland, a Presbyterian form of Protestantism, is more democratic than the Church of England. Even in Catholicism, Scotland is recognised by the Vatican as a separate entity, headed by its own cardinal, while the Episcopal Church in Scotland may be in communion with Anglicanism but has its own identity.

The vast majority of Scots may speak English with a variety of regional accents, but there has been a dramatic resurgence in recent years of both Scots and Gaelic. Scots, spoken in the Lowlands, developed as a separate branch of English and attained its zenith as a literary language in the fifteenth and sixteenth centuries. However, it went into decline from the Reformation of 1560 onwards. Attempts to revive it in its literary form began in the eighteenth century, but it is only within recent years that it has really flourished in prose, poetry and plays. As the everyday vernacular of the Scots, it has shown a remarkable resilience in the face of the dominance of English in radio and television.

So, too, Gaelic, once the language of the Highlands and Islands, had been in decline since the eighteenth century but now – thanks to a generous amount of time on Scottish national radio and television, as well as a dedicated service of its own in Radio nan Eilean – this ancient Celtic tongue is making a comeback. Significantly, its use in street signs, shop signs and railway stations has increased enormously in recent years, an immediately apparent reflection of Scottish awareness of their separate identity.

The other side of the coin is that Scotland and the Scots are inextricably part of the island of Great Britain and politically a component of the United Kingdom. It has been estimated that expatriate Scots, and people of Scots descent, are six times more numerous than the people living in Scotland itself. The Scottish diaspora is as widespread as its Jewish counterpart: consult the telephone book in any part of the world and you will be amazed at the number of Scottish names.

Consider the Scottish contribution to the political life of the United Kingdom. Scotland has provided 11 prime ministers: the Marquis of Bute, the Earl of Aberdeen, Lord Rosebery, Arthur Balfour, Sir Henry Campbell Bannerman, Ramsay Macdonald and Sir Alec Douglas-Home were actually born there. William Ewart Gladstone was born in Liverpool and Andrew Bonar Law in New Brunswick, Canada, but both had Scottish parents, while Harold Macmillan and Tony Blair are of Scots descent.

Scots took the lead in the development of socialism. Keir Hardie, descended from one of the martyrs of the 1820 uprising, was the first workingman to take his place in the House of Commons and was a founder of the Labour Party, while the pioneer socialist John Maclean was

▲ *Ramsay MacDonald*

so highly thought of by Lenin that he was appointed first Bolshevik Consul in Britain. To this day, the rugged radicalism of the Scots can be seen in the leadership of many of the trade unions.

At the other end of the political spectrum, countless Scots have attained cabinet rank. Just consider the front-bench line-up in recent years. You would find on one side Norman Lamont, Malcolm Rifkind and Ian Lang, while at the present time there are Gordon Brown, George Robertson, Donald Dewar and Robin Cook. Tony Blair inherited the leadership of the Labour Party from John Smith from  Argyll, while his predecessor, Neil Kinnock, was born in Wales of Scottish parents. The present Lord Chancellor, Lord Irvine of Lairg, and his immediate predecessor, Lord Mackay of Clashfern, are both Scots.

Looking farther afield, we find that 20 US presidents had Scottish blood in their veins, while the signatories of the Declaration of Independence included James Wilson from Fife and John Witherspoon from East Lothian. Between them, John Macdonald (from Glasgow) and Alexander Mackenzie (from Perthshire) alternately held the premiership of Canada from the inception of the Confederation in 1867 till 1891, apart for a very brief spell when George Brown (from Edinburgh) was prime minister. Andrew Fisher from Kilmarnock was three times prime minister of Australia.

The Scots as empire builders have an astonishing record in relation to the size of the population. James Cook, born in Yorkshire of Scottish parents, gave Britain the prospect of an empire in the South Pacific, though it was administrators like Lachlan Macquarie from Mull who

▲ *Norman Lamont*

developed it. English-speaking Canada was largely explored and settled by Scots. The Hudson Bay Company recruited mainly in Orkney, though its most famous employee, Donald Smith (later Lord Strathcona) hailed from Moray. Leander Starr Jameson, who led the raid into the Transvaal which sparked off the Boer War, hailed from Edinburgh.

The Scottish contribution to the spread of Christianity is also impressive, from St Patrick (born at Dumbarton) to David Livingstone (from Blantyre). Missionaries like Mary Slessor, Robert Moffat and John Love, who helped to found the London Missionary Society, are but a few of the men and women who spread the gospel to every corner of the globe. In 1868, Archibald Campbell Tait from Edinburgh became Archbishop of Canterbury, and in the course of the twentieth century Randall Davidson from Muirhouse near Edinburgh and Cosmo Gordon Lang from Aberdeenshire would also hold the highest office in the Church of England.

In the profession of arms the Scots have an impressive record. A warlike people since Roman times, when not feuding among themselves they proved to be formidable opponents. Though it has to be admitted that in bloody encounters with the old enemy the Scots were seldom a match for the heavier armed and highly disciplined English, they proved the better side at Stirling Bridge and Bannockburn. In the seventeenth century the martial prowess of the Scots was greatly prized by the kings of France and Sweden. Many of the great soldiers of the eighteenth and nineteenth centuries, from

▲ *St Patrick*

Etienne Macdonald in France to Prince Barclay de Tolly in Russia, were of Scottish descent. Thomas Cochrane, Earl of Dundonald, headed the navies of Chile, Peru and Greece as well as being an admiral in the Royal Navy. John Paul Jones from Kirkcudbrightshire, founder of the United States Navy, also served as an admiral under Catherine the Great in the Black Sea campaign against the Turks, while his compatriot, Samuel Greig, led the Russian Navy in the Baltic.

It goes without saying that Scotland has contributed more than its share of field marshals to the British Army, while two of the marshals of the Royal Air Force in World War II were Hugh Dowding (from Dumfriesshire) and Arthur Tedder (from Stirlingshire).

Perhaps on account of its superior educational system, with compulsory attendance at parish schools from 1694 onwards, Scotland's contribution to science and medicine, engineering and invention, has been outstanding. James Watt (steam-power), James Clerk Maxwell (physics), William Murdock (gaslight), Alexander Graham Bell (the telephone), John Napier (logarithms), John Boyd Dunlop (the pneumatic tyre), John Logie Baird (television), Sir James Young Simpson (anaesthesia) and

▲ *Bannockburn*   *Tony Blair* ▶

Alexander Fleming (penicillin) are only a few of the great names which have become household words. Scottish inventions, from the bicycle to beta-blockers, have enriched the world in myriad ways. Adam Smith from Kirkcaldy is the father of economics, while Alan Pinkerton from Glasgow was the original 'private eye'. In the field of civil engineering Thomas Telford and John Rennie built the canals, harbours, bridges and docks that revolutionised the transport system of Britain, while John Loudon Macadam transformed road-building throughout the world and gave the word 'tarmac' to the English language.

In the arts and literature, the Scottish element may not be correspondingly great, but Scotland was the birthplace of Burns and Scott, of Robert Louis Stevenson, J.M. Barrie and John Buchan, while Byron, 'born half a Scot, was bred a whole one'. Raeburn, Ramsay and Wilkie were among the foremost portrait-painters of their day, while the Glasgow Boys played a prominent part in artistic development in the nineteenth and early twentieth centuries. The Adam brothers revolutionised architecture in the eighteenth century, just as Charles Rennie Mackintosh was a major influence in architecture and interior design in Europe at the beginning of the twentieth century.

The canny Scot may be a stereotype, but it was a Scot, William Paterson from Dumfries, who founded the Bank of England (1694) and the Bank of

▲ *Charles Rennie Mackintosh bedroom*

Scotland (1695), and another, John Law, who founded the Banque de France (1720). The Revd Henry Duncan of Ruthwell founded the world's first savings bank (1810). A canny Scot who became one of the world's richest men and ended up by giving away most of his vast fortune was Dunfermline-born Andrew Carnegie, whose name is a byword for philanthropy to this day.

Scotland has its own distinctive culture and traditions, from Highland Games and Burns Suppers to Scotch whisky, haggis, tartan, kilts and bagpipes, but these are only the superficial manifestations of a way of life that

is different from that found in England. It is also, regrettably, evident in the relatively poor health of the Scots, who have one of the highest incidences of heart disease in Europe, despite several attempts by successive governments to improve the Scottish diet.

The Scots invented golf and curling and have a long tradition of excellence on the football pitch – except when it comes to the World Cup, in which the national team regularly qualifies but seldom progresses beyond the first round. Still, the very existence of a Scottish team, competing against Brazil, Norway, France or Germany on equal terms, is somehow symbolic. In spite of almost 300 years in the shadow of her powerful neighbour, Scotland continues to have a separate identity and a distinctive character. It has also had a long, and at times very turbulent, history.

Highland games ▲

Mesolithic Hunters and Fishermen

THE EARLIEST HUMAN INHABITANTS of whom there is any trace moved north into what is now Scotland in about 7000 BC during the Mesolithic (Middle Stone Age) period.

THESE PEOPLE clung to the deeply indented coasts of the west of Scotland and the islands of the Inner Hebrides, subsisting on inshore spear-fishing and shellfish gathered from rocks and reefs. To go inland meant forest and swamp, and so they seldom penetrated far into the heavily wooded hinterland; when they did it was in pursuit of wild animals, which provided them not just with meat and hides but also with bone or antlers, from which they were able to fashion primitive harpoons. By about 6000 BC they were also using flint tools, originally for scraping skins, and later larger implements with a sharpened edge, suitable for cutting wood. The people were nomadic, probably moving from place to place, as they went in search of food, perhaps moving with the change of the seasons. No evidence of permanent settlements has been found, but their campsites and rubbish dumps have, in recent years, enabled archaeologists to form a clearer picture of their activities, while techniques such as carbon-dating have provided a more precise chronology.

A group of three stone rings at Lussa Wood on the island of Jura is regarded as the earliest stone structure in Scotland, and it is thought that these may have been the bases for tents made of hides. Mesolithic deposits, such as shell mounds and middens, have been found on Oronsay, Kintyre and Luce Bay on the west coast, and in Fife, Deeside and the Forth estuary on the east.

▲ *Iron Age hunters with their tools*

Neolithic Farmers

WHILE THE MESOLITHIC HUNTERS left little mark on the land, the people who came afterwards in the Neolithic (New Stone Age) period formed permanent settlements, clearing forest and tilling the soil, planting seed and harvesting crops.

▲ *A Neolithic farmer*

THE EARLIEST settlements, about 4000 BC, were on low-lying coasts. Unfortunately, rising sea levels after the last Ice Age have obliterated much of the evidence, though enough remains to suggest that the Neolithic people came to Scotland by sea.

There is no doubt that they built timber houses, but because of the perishable nature of wood they are best remembered for about a dozen hamlets consisting of clusters of stone structures built in areas where timber would have been scarce. Thus the remarkable settlement at Skara Brae in Orkney, engulfed by sand and therefore preserved intact for thousands of years until uncovered by Gordon Childe in 1927, may convey a false impression that all Neolithic settlers lived in this manner. Elsewhere, post-holes and stone hearths indicate the presence of wooden houses.

Apart from a dozen stone settlements, the Neolithic people are most memorable for their burial customs, interring their dead in elaborate chambered tombs, cairns, long barrows, passage graves and burial mounds which have yielded a wide range of grave goods accompanying the deceased to the afterlife.

Five major types of chambered tomb have been classified according to their structure; Clyde cairns (Argyll and Arran), and the passage graves of the Bargrennan, Clava, Maes Howe and Orkney types.

▲ *Skara Brae, Orkney*

Stone Circles and Alignments

SOME OF THE EARLY SETTLERS have been labelled Megalithic (Large Stone) because of their propensity to erect massive stone monuments. Whereas cairns and chambered tombs are also found in many parts of Continental Europe, these standing stones are peculiar to the British Isles.

T HE USUAL pattern was a large ditch surrounded by an outer bank of earth, the whole encircling a ring of giant monoliths. Sometimes there were concentric rings of standing stones, with an outer circle of timber posts. The latter have long since disappeared, betrayed only by post-holes and vestigial organic material, but the stones themselves form an impressive sight to this day.

Though Scotland has nothing that quite compares with Stonehenge in Wiltshire, England, the west coast of Lewis in the Outer Hebrides comes close. Dramatic when silhouetted against a Hebridean sunset, it

▲ *Callanish Standing Stones, Lewis*

is even more remarkable from the air, from which viewpoint the cruciform arrangement of the columns radiating from the central circle can best be appreciated. Other henges which are prominent landmarks include the Ring of Brodgar and the Stones of Stenness (both in Orkney), and a number of stone alignments in Argyll which indicate an appreciation of the movements of the sun and moon. Some of the stones weigh up to three tonnes; a considerable weight, especially for a people who were without the use of levers or rollers to help them.

Ring of Brodgar, Orkney ▲

There are also many isolated monoliths, sometimes decorated with cup and ring marks or concentric whorls, as well as the recumbent stone circles, the latter being mainly confined to the Buchan and central districts of Aberdeenshire. Much remains to be discovered about the people who erected these strange structures and where they acquired their engineering skills.

Beaker People

ABOUT 2500 BC there began a wave of migration from Europe, possibly the Low Countries, of people who are noted for their earthenware pottery from which they are known as the Beaker People. Though this is something of a misnomer, it remains a convenient label for these incomers who flourished till about 1500 BC.

THE BEAKERS range from small slender vessels – drinking vessels for mead or beer – to large urns and food containers, usually with a bell-shaped mouth, sometimes a waist and a bulbous body, though others had a wide top, tapered body and narrow base. They were notable for their incised decoration in a wide variety of geometric patterns. They have been classified into several types, according to such features as all-over-cord decoration and 'European' bell shape. From the incidence of the various types, some scholars have advanced theories concerning different waves of migration from the Continent, perhaps originating in Spain, while others regard the different styles as merely evidence of a gradual evolution by peoples who were already well established: they could also be nothing other than a status symbol, disseminated by trade and copied locally. It is likely that the development of beaker pottery arose from a combination of these circumstances.

Most of the intact specimens were recovered from burial chambers and were believed to contain food and drink for the next world. This theory is bolstered by the fact that they were often interred with crouched corpses in stone cists. Later, however, cremation was widely practised, and the ashes were often interred in cinerary urns. The Beaker People settled on the east coast of Scotland and gradually moved inland.

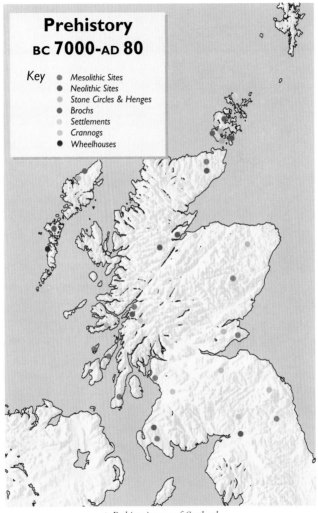

Prehistory
BC **7000**-AD **80**

Key
- Mesolithic Sites
- Neolithic Sites
- Stone Circles & Henges
- Brochs
- Settlements
- Crannogs
- Wheelhouses

▲ *Prehistoric map of Scotland*

The Bronze Age

From the presence of some bronze ornaments and implements – such as metal axes with wooden handles, and bronze daggers – in the graves of the Beaker People, it seems that they had a rudimentary acquaintance with metalworking, although this did not become widespread until about 2000 BC.

THE USE OF BRONZE appears to have spread to Scotland from Ireland, where there was an abundance of copper and tin, and where a knowledge of metallurgy developed early. The earliest bronze tools and implements consisted of axes, spears and halberds, but there was also a fashion for personal adornment in the form of bronze earrings, armlets, bracelets, brooches and necklaces.

The earliest bronze artefacts were cast in open moulds carved from stone. By the Middle Bronze Age (1400 BC–900 BC) tools and weapons were much more technically accomplished, being cast in closed sand moulds which permitted the development of socketed axes, spears and palstaves. The most powerful were fond of displaying their

▲ *Deer-hunting in the Bronze Age*

wealth, and decoration of bronze articles was now achieved by chisels and punches, while sheet bronze was fashioned with hammers on an anvil.

By the Late Bronze Age (about 900 BC–400 BC), metalworkers were producing elaborate shields, cauldrons and pots, as well as daggers, short swords and even razors.

▲ *Bronze Age metal founders*

Associated with the bronze artefacts are the gold torques, discs, armlets and lunular chest ornaments. Beads of jet or amber are also known from the Early Bronze Age period and indicate that the inhabitants of Scotland traded not only with Ireland and Cornwall but also with Scandinavia and the Low Countries.

Iron Age

BY 500 BC, iron was beginning to replace bronze as the preferred metal for tools and weapons, although the transition was gradual. It is probable that the use of iron, a harder metal capable of taking a sharper edge, coincided with the first waves of Celtic migration. The Celts were the first race to use the long sword and small shield.

T HE EXISTING Bronze Age peoples of Scotland were forced on the defensive by incursions of these newcomers from Europe. It is significant that many of the Bronze Age hoards date from the period of the sixth and seventh centuries BC when people buried their precious posessions in face of invasion.

To the same period belongs the erection of the earliest fortifications, intended to withstand the onslaught. Settlements, such as the one found in East Lothian, had to be fortified as tribal warfare became a way of life for the Caledonians. These timber palisades interspersed with stones, erected on hilltops, provided an excellent vantage point as well as a good defensive position. Sometimes the attackers set fire to these forts with the result that the stones were fused by the extreme heat. Such vitrified remains have been found on many hilltops, the best examples being at Kaimes Hill (Midlothian) and Traprain Law and Eildon Hill North (both Roxburghshire).

Palisades were also used to enclose farms and homesteads, and even clusters of houses. There might also be an outer enclosure for sheep or cattle. Good examples may be seen at Broxmouth (East Lothian), Greenborough Hill and Hayhope Knowe (both Roxburghshire), and Burnswark (Dumfriesshire). Many of the forts, in fact, developed out of palisaded homesteads.

◄ *Iron Age agriculture*

Celtic Migrations

ABOUT 900 BC the first wave of Celtic migration took place. The Celts spread westward across Europe, through southern Germany, France and Belgium, and crossed the Channel to colonise Britain and Ireland.

THEIR ANCIENT Indo-European language divided into two branches which linguists classify as P-Celtic or Brythonic (represented by Welsh, Cornish and Breton), and Q-Celtic or Goidelic (represented by Scottish, Irish and Manx Gaelic). The division centres on the use of P or Q sounds in otherwise similar words, such as head (ceann in Gaelic and pen in Welsh).

These people – who were skilled in working iron – decorated their faces and bodies with dyes. In Goidelic they called themselves Cruithne (the painted ones) but in Brythonic this became Pruithne, hence Brythonic itself, and eventually Breatan or Briton. Centuries later, the Romans – when they penetrated North Britain – would call the wild inhabitants Picti (which means 'painted'), a race whose memory is perpetuated in placenames beginning

A Celtic statue ▶

with Pit (Pitcur, Pitmeddan, Pitarrow) or Pent (from the Pentland Firth to the Pentland Hills).

The Goidelic Celts settled in Ireland and probably colonised western Scotland from there. The Brythonic Celts occupied eastern Scotland, from the Forth estuary to Orkney and Shetland.

It seems probable that Celtic society in Scotland followed the same pattern as elsewhere (e.g. Gaul). Family, clan or tribal units would be headed by chieftains and eventually petty kings. A tribal aristocracy, drawn from the best warriors, also emerged, with a middle class of druids (priests) and bards, followed by tenant farmers, artisans and bondsmen (slaves).

▲ *A cauldron displaying Celtic icons*

Crannogs

A CRANNOG IS A STRUCTURE, usually of wood, erected on an artificial island close to the shore of a loch and connected to the bank by a narrow causeway. They were built for defence from about 400 BC onwards and survived into the Christian era. The etymology of the word is unknown, although it survives in modern Gaelic as 'crannag', a pulpit or perch.

CRANNOGS were built to defend against both animal and human invaders (the humans, though not yet Vikings, coming from the sea). The islands themselves were formed out of great heaps of stones and boulders on top of which were placed logs criss-cross fashion, interspersed with turf and brushwood, the whole pinned together with timber piles and revetted with large rocks. They were effective protection. Some have vanished beneath the surface as the water level has risen; others have become stranded in areas which have been drained; but many survive more or less as they were more than 2000 years ago. The timber edifice, of course, has long since disappeared and the rocky islet may be heavily overgrown with trees, shrubs and vegetation, but the telltale rock mounds and remains of a causeway betray their original purpose.

They are to be found all over Scotland, from North Uist to Kirkcudbrightshire. An aerial survey of Loch Awe revealed 20 crannogs, most of which are underwater. From the thick muddy deposits at the base of crannogs has emerged a wealth of material dating between about 400 BC and 200 AD, including clothing, leather footwear, canoes and even wooden ploughs. A crannog at Hyndford, Lanarkshire contained glassware and Roman artefacts indicating occupancy as late as the end of the first century AD.

▲ *A crannog on Loch Eilt*

Brochs

BROCHS (FROM THE SCOTS WORD 'burgh', a borough) are circular fortified towers dating from about 100 BC to AD 300, although the Broch of Mousa was still being used as a refuge in the Viking era. The remains of about 500 have been recorded in the north and west of Scotland, including the Outer Hebrides and the Northern Isles. They are unique to Scotland and have no counterpart anywhere else.

▲ *The Broch of Gurness, Orkney*

APART FROM that, they are remarkable in the standardisation of their construction, considering their widespread distribution (and, similar to crannogs, were successful in their role of defence). This has given rise to the notion that they were all built by a team of engineers who travelled from place to place and passed on their skills to others who copied their design over a period of about 200 years.

Many of them have since been eroded over time and survive as little more than foundations and the remains of walls, but sufficient is there to show the characteristic circular ground plan and hollow walls. Among the better preserved examples, such as the brochs at Dun Carloway in Lewis and Clickhimin in Shetland, the massive base and sloping walls, the interior galleries and wall cells follow a set pattern.

The finest extant example, the Broch of Mousa in Shetland, attains a height of 13 m (40 ft). Almost two-thirds of its overall diameter is taken up with masonry, with a narrow central space and small chambers radiating from it. The hollow wall consisted of inner and outer walls bonded at intervals by horizontal slabs which formed a series of internal galleries. A spiral stone staircase wound its way up from ground level to the ramparts.

▲ *Dun Carloway Broch, Lewis*

Duns, Souterrains and Wheelhouses

OTHER FORMS OF DWELLING from the prehistoric Celtic period include duns, souterrains and wheelhouses. The first of these (from Gaelic dun, a fort) is often used loosely to describe the remains of any thick-walled compound to which the extended family could retire in times of attack, but the others were designed for permanent occupation.

DUNS, AS FORTIFIED PLACES, were prominent landmarks which are enshrined in innumerable placenames all over Scotland. Most of them were erected on rocky eminences which made them easier to defend or on narrow promontories with a wall across the landward side, as in the strange structure which gives the island of Dun, St Kilda its name. Duns are scattered all over Scotland, although they predominate in Argyll where there are many well-preserved examples to this day.

Souterrains, as their name suggests, are underground dwellings. Basically they were a hole in the ground, lined and paved with stone, only their sloping timber and thatched roofs sticking above ground level. They were in use from about 100 BC to AD 100. After they were abandoned, their roofs collapsed and they were often engulfed by shifting sand. About 200 have been recorded, mostly in the Western Isles, Skye, Orkney, Shetland, Sutherland, Ross, Aberdeenshire, Angus and Perthshire.

They should not be confused with the wheelhouses found in the Western Isles, so called because their ground plan is wheel-shaped, with a hearth at the hub and chambers divided by radial walls like spokes.

▲ *Broch and Souterrains at Carn Liath, Sutherland*

Roman Period, AD 80–401

THE PREHISTORY OF SCOTLAND ended abruptly in AD 80 when the Roman general Agricola, on the orders of the Emperor Titus and with a force of 20,000 men, led an expedition into southern Scotland and reached the Tay estuary. There he proceeded to build fortifications to keep out the northern tribesmen, while his Roman fleet supplied him from the Channel. His exploits were chronicled by his son-in-law, Tacitus, who provides us with the first written record of the country which the Romans called Caledonia.

SOUTHERN BRITAIN had been visited by Julius Caesar in 55–54 BC and conquered by the Romans under Claudius in AD 43. Within four years Roman rule covered all the land south of the Severn and the Trent. Despite such setbacks as the revolt of the Iceni under Boudicca (Boadicea) in AD 61 and the defection of the Brigantes of Yorkshire in AD 68, the Romans pushed northwards relentlessly. In AD 78, Wales was subjugated and the Romans turned their attention to the north of Britain.

The Roman advance in AD 81 was two-pronged, one column heading through Annandale and down the Clyde valley while the other marched along the east coast route into the Lothians. Along these lines of advance the first Roman roads were laid, with forts and guardhouses at strategic intervals. Agricola easily subjugated the Lowland tribes and over a period of 14 months established a network of forts (see p. 40) across the isthmus of the Forth and Clyde, linked by military roads.

From the main north-south roads Agricola's troops fanned out in all

Roman map of Scotland ▶

directions. The wilderness of Galloway was controlled by forts at Glenlochar and Dalswinton, while a number of forts were manned in the foothills of the mountains at Fendoch, Bochastle, Malling and other points in Perthshire. This phase of operations was completed by the erection of a great legionary fortress at Inchtuthil near modern Dunkeld.

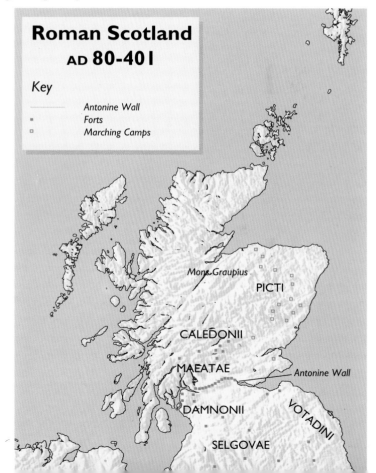

Roman Scotland
AD 80-401

Key

―――	Antonine Wall
▪	Forts
▫	Marching Camps

Mons Graupius

PICTI

CALEDONII

MAEATAE

Antonine Wall

DAMNONII

VOTADINI

SELGOVAE

Mons Graupius

TITUS WAS DETERMINED to bring the whole of Britain under Roman rule. In 83 he ordered Agricola to advance north of the Tay and subjugate the Picts.

UNLIKE THE INVASION of the South, the Roman penetration of Pictland did not go unchallenged. Tacitus used his battle fleet to harass the coast and the following year confronted the Picts in a great pitched battle at a place which Tacitus called Mons Graupius. It is believed that the battle was fought at Bennachie in central Aberdeenshire. Here, the Ninth Legion (numbering a total of 5,000 men) decisively defeated an army of 30,000 led by Calgacus, 'the swordsman', the first Scottish person

whose name has come down to posterity. The Romans were expert and professional soldiers, and had been fighting as a unit for centuries, hence their advantage despite the odds working against them.

In his vivid account of the battle, Tacitus reports verbatim the rousing speech delivered by Calgacus to his troops, ending with the memorable words *solitudinem faciunt pacem appellant*, 'They make a desert and they call it peace'. These bitter words show that the Pictish leader had the measure of Imperial Rome. They would be just as appropriate in describing the armies of Edward I in 1296 or the 'Rough Wooing' of Mary,

▲ *Roman coins*

Queen of Scots in 1543–45.

The Picts proved no match for the close-order combat of the legionaries. Calgacus was killed and his warriors decimated, but the Romans soon found Caledonia to be impossible to pacify. Agricola contented himself with sending his fleet to chart the northern coasts while he and his troops withdrew to Inchtuthil. From freshly minted coins found there, it seems that Agricola abandoned this fortress precipitately about 86.

▲ *Bennachie, site of the battle of Mons Graupius*

Occupation of Southern Scotland to AD 105

IT IS BELIEVED THAT, following the abandonment of Inchtuthil, the Romans erected a series of watchtowers from Ardoch to Bertha, but these, in turn, were evacuated about 90. Temporary campsites have been located by aerial survey in recent years. Some may date from the Agricolan campaign but others may relate to campaigns under Septimius Severus in the early third century.

NEWSTEAD IN Roxburghshire was considerably extended at the end of the first century, assuming new importance as the spearhead of any future Roman incursion into the Scottish Lowlands. Compared with the unfinished nature of Inchtuthil, Newstead was built to last, with robust stone-built barrack blocks and a mass of ancillary buildings. In the end, however, the town's occupation proved to be only temporary.

Newstead, Dalswinton, Glenlochar and a few other forts

Roman parade helmet ▶

probably continued to be garrisoned till about 105, when the Romans withdrew south of a line from the Solway to the Tyne. It is not known what caused this withdrawal but possibly the loss of the Ninth Legion, which disappeared without trace (one theory is that the Caledonians filled the bodies of the dead Romans with stones and sank them into the loch), may have been the reason. In 121, Hadrian erected the great wall which still bears his name, running between Carlisle and South Shields. The wall was designed to keep out the tribesmen who continued to invade Roman-occupied lands. It was up to 3 m (10 ft) broad at its base and over 2 m (6 ft) across at the top. Over 14,000 men laboured in its construction. The eastern end of this mighty bulwark was faced with masonry, but the scheme was never completed and the western end was dressed with clay and turf only.

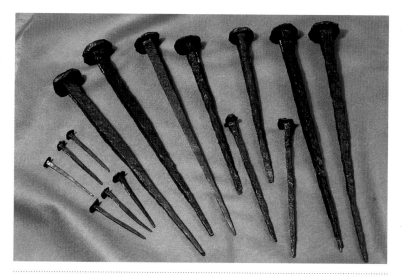

▲ *Roman nails from Inchtuthil Fort*

The Antonine Wall

THE RECONQUEST of southern Scotland by Lollius Urbicus (139–42) was completed by the construction of a new wall, across the isthmus of the Forth and Clyde, named in honour of the Emperor Antoninus Pius.

THE WALL CUT Caledonia off from the rest of already occupied lower Britain, and ran from Old Kilpatrick in Dunbartonshire to Bridgeness near Carriden, Stirlingshire on the Firth of Forth, a distance of 40 Roman miles (57 km or 36 statute miles). The wall followed the line of the earlier Agricolan forts and consisted of a turf earthwork standing 3 m (10 ft) high, on a stone foundation 4.3 m (14 ft) wide. On the north side of the wall ran a deep ditch with a counterscarp embankment on its outer edge. South of the wall and running alongside it for 72 km (45 miles) was a military road, extending in both directions to outlying forts beyond the ends of the wall itself.

Along the wall were located 20 forts at regular intervals of approximately 3.2 km (two miles), with another 12 outposts in the surrounding countryside, as far north as Malling in Perthshire near the headwaters of the Forth. The wall was constructed by troops of the Second, Sixth and Twelfth Legions, who celebrated completion of their sections with commemorative stone slabs. The best-preserved of the forts is at Rough Castle near Bonnybridge.

After the death of Antoninus Pius in 161 the garrisons were withdrawn to Hadrian's Wall, though some forts were manned intermittently

A distance slab, originally set into the Antonine Wall ▶

thereafter. The legacy the forts left was to have helped unify the tribes of Scotland by the Romans attempting to conquer them.

Campaigns of Septimius Severus

AFTER 161, Roman tactics seem to have been merely to patrol the Lowlands with a view to keeping the tribes in check and give warning of any attempt by them to breach Hadrian's Wall. For almost half a century this policy worked well enough.

EARLY IN THE third century, however, the tribes became increasingly troublesome. Their marauding expeditions became bolder and attacks on the wall more frequent. In the end, an exasperated Roman governor pleaded with the Emperor Septimius Severus to send reinforcements. The Emperor went a step further by coming over to Britain in person to superintend a campaign aimed at putting the troublesome Picts in their place.

▲ *Hadrian's Wall*

Accompanied by his sons Caracalla and Geta, the Emperor went to Britain. In the summer of 208 the imperial entourage travelled north and established a great naval base at Cramond on the Forth. Detailed plans for creating lines of communication and provisioning a vast expedition were laid and a new legionary fortress was constructed at Carpow on the bank of the Tay, with a subsidiary camp at Keithock in Angus.

The Caledonii and Maeatae were overawed by these belligerent preparations and were forced to negotiate with the Septimius Severus. The treaty was short-lived, however, for the Maeatae rose in rebellion, shortly followed by the Caledonii. Caracalla advanced as far as Stonehaven but the campaign ended in AD 211 with the death of Severus. Caracalla and Geta immediately hurried back to Rome to contest the imperial throne and the campaign in southern Scotland fizzled out. Carpow was evacuated and demolished the following year.

▲ *Hadrian orders a wall to exclude the Scots*

Final Roman Campaigns in Scotland

ALTHOUGH THE Romans practically abandoned Britain north of
Hadrian's Wall in 212, there were periodic campaigns until 401.

BY THE THIRD century a clearer picture of the inhabitants of
Scotland was beginning to emerge. The tribes who lived south of the
Forth and Clyde isthmus were regarded by the Romans as kin to
those in Roman Britain. They spoke the same Brythonic language and
were more amenable to a Roman presence than the fierce Maeatae and
Caledonii of the north. Roman writers differentiate between the
Damnonii of the Clyde valley, the Novantae of the far south-west, the
Selgovae of the Tweed valley and the Votadini of the Lothians.

These tribes tolerated Roman incursions, unlike the troublesome

▲ *Leaderfoot viaduct – the site of Trimontium, the Roman Empire's most northern amphitheatre*

Picti and Hiberni described by Eumenius in 297 as enemies of the Britons. The Hiberni or Scoti were Celts, speaking a Goidelic tongue, the ancestor of modern Gaelic. There is considerable confusion regarding the language of the Picts, which is described as an older form of Celtic or even a language so ancient that it was neither Celtic nor Indo-European.

An alliance of Picts, Scots, Attacotti and Saxon pirates attacked Roman Britain in 364. After a series of continued attacks by these barbarians, the Emperor Valentinian was goaded into sending Theodosius to Britain, in 367, to combat this menace. In a vigorous campaign the following year, Theodosius restored the Pax Romana (or Roman rule) as far north as the Tyne-Solway line. In 382, Magnus Maximus took the war into the enemy's heartland, but he did not subdue them and, by 394, the Picts and Scots were on the rampage again. Stilicho subdued them in 396 but was forced to withdraw his troops in 401 to face the Goths. A combination of boredom and common sense had eventually persuaded the Empire to leave Scotland to the natives.

The Coming of Christianity, 397–664

IN 325, CONSTANTINE the Great had made Christianity the official religion of the Roman Empire and it spread as far as the province of Britain. About the middle of the century there was born one Ringan, or Ninian, son of Romano-British parents who had converted to the new faith.

NINIAN WAS BORN around 350 and, as a young man, he journeyed to Rome; later he spent some time at Tours where he came under the spiritual influence of St Martin. He returned to Britain in 397 and settled on the Solway coast near present-day Whithorn where he founded a monastery known as Candida Casa (Latin for 'white house', because it was built of whitewashed stone). Monastic cells at the Isle of Whithorn and St Ninian's Cave farther along the coast testify to the ascetic nature of his mission, with its emphasis on the hermit's way of life.

From this modest beginning, Christianity gradually spread northwards throughout Galloway and Strathclyde at a time when the Romans had evacuated southern Britain and the Dark Ages were

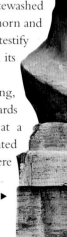

Constantine the Great ▶

descending on the former Roman province. Candida Casa became an important centre of learning, an oasis in a pagan wilderness. Here Ninian and his acolytes trained monks in the liturgy of St Ambrose. Ninian followed the practice established by the Council of Arles (314) for the computing of the date of Easter, and his followers remained true to this, even though Rome changed the calendar twice in the fifth and once in the sixth century. By the time of his death in 432, Ninian had spread the Gospel throughout Strathclyde and had even sent missionaries into eastern Scotland; his followers may have taken the new faith as far north as the Shetland Islands.

▲ *The remains of Candida Casa*

Patrick and Columba

PATRICIUS OR PATRICK was born at Dumbarton ('the fort of the Britons') about 389. In 405 he was taken prisoner in a raid by the Irish king, Niall Noigiallach, and sold into slavery in Antrim.

HE ESCAPED IN 411 and made his way to Gaul, where he lived for several years before returning to Britain. A deeply religious man, he had a dream that an angel named Victor called him to convert the heathen of Ireland. In 432, he was sent to Ireland by Pope Germanus, and for 30 years he worked tirelessly to convert the Irish to Christianity, founding convents, monasteries and churches. In 461, he died at Saul in Dalriada (northern Ireland).

Born in 521 at Gartan, Co. Donegal, Columba belonged to the Hy Neill, the reigning house of Ulster and Dalriada. He studied for the priesthood under Finian of Moville and was ordained about 551. Over the ensuing decade he founded churches and monasteries in various parts of Ireland, but in 563 he sailed eastward with 12 disciples and settled on the island of Iona, where he erected a church and a monastery.

The early mission of Ninian had long since vanished without trace, and thus it fell to Columba and his followers to re-establish Christianity. Eventually he reached Inverness, the capital of the kingdom of King Brude. After a miracle-working contest with the local pagan priests, Columba convinced Brude that his was the true religion. Brude converted to Christianity and his Pictish subjects dutifully followed suit. As statesman and administrator, Columba played a notable part in the foundation

St Patrick ▶

of Scotland. He died at Iona in 597, having helped the Scots to establish Argyll in western Scotland as an independent kingdom. by using his new faith and royal connections.

St Kentigern

ABOUT 584, Columba began his mission to the people who lived in the Tay valley. It was soon afterwards that he had his celebrated meeting with Kentigern, whose missionary endeavours were then expanding northwards from Glasgow into Stirlingshire and Perthshire.

▲ *St Columba*

KENTIGERN, better known to posterity by his nickname of Mungo ('dear friend'), had a bad start in life, early in the sixth century. When the Pictish princess Tanew or Tannoch was found to have given birth though unwed, her enraged father had her and the infant hurled from the top of his fortress on Traprain Law. Mother and baby miraculously escaped the ordeal and fled westward, receiving sanctuary at St Ninian's chapel in Glasgow. In due course the boy was ordained and eventually became bishop of the city. His mother, after her unfortunate early lapse, became renowned for her piety and was later canonised. St Enoch, in the heart of Glasgow, is a corruption of her name, St Tannoch.

Kentigern is almost as shadowy a figure as Ninian, remembered chiefly for the four miracles symbolised in the arms of the city of Glasgow, of which he is the patron saint. He was forced to flee to Wales, where he took refuge with St David at Menevia and later founded the monastery of St Asaph's. When King Rhydderch defeated the pagans at the battle of Arderydd in 573, Kentigern returned to Strathclyde, fixing his see at Hoddam in Dumfriesshire before moving to Glasgow and laying the foundations of the great cathedral that stands to this day. Kentigern died in 612.

▲ *The arms of the City of Glasgow*

Missionary Activity

UNDER COLUMBA and his successors, Iona became a place of pilgrimage and the cemetery of many kings, not only of the petty kingdoms of Scotland and Ireland but as far afield as Norway and France.

MORE IMPORTANTLY, this tiny offshore island became the training centre for monks who took the Celtic version of Christianity as far as central Europe. While Kilian, Totnan and Colman converted the heathen in Franconia and Suabia (now southern Germany), St Gall preached in the valleys of Switzerland.

Nearer home, Moluag and Maelrubba worked among the Picts, consolidating earlier missions, while Aidan, who established himself on Holy Island near Bamburgh, launched the great mission that led to the conversion of the heathen Angles of Northumbria in the seventh century. Aidan also founded the monastery at Melrose, from where St Cuthbert conducted his mission to the Angles of Lothian.

The Celtic Church was monastic and spiritual, unlike the great religious houses that were to come to Scotland in the Middle Ages. The Celtic Church was extremely strict, demanding poverty and obedience from its clergy, however it lacked any real structure. For instance, there were no parishes or bishoprics with a clearly defined hierarchy, as were found in later Churches. Such authority as there was depended on the abbots of individual monasteries, but the itinerant monks, most of whom lived in isolated cells, worked on their own and therefore had little contact with one another. Sworn to poverty and obedience but not to

Cross on Iona ▶

chastity, many of the monks took wives. Tiny churches and chapels were erected in a haphazard fashion, while observance of the sacraments varied considerably from one district to another. Above all else, it was in the date on which Easter was celebrated that the Celtic Church differed from its Roman counterpart.

The Synod of Whitby

NOTHING CONCENTRATES the minds of men more than natural disasters. In 664, an earthquake, a solar eclipse and a devastating outbreak of the plague betokened God's displeasure. The outcome was the calling of the Synod of Whitby by Oswy, King of Northumbria.

AT THIS GREAT ecclesiastical gathering there was a showdown between the Celtic monks and their Roman rivals. Pagan England had gradually been won back to Christianity since the landing of Augustine in Kent in 597. Indeed, for a time in the early seventh century, Paulinus from York had converted the Angles of Northumbria but this had been undone by the defeat of King Edwin in 633. As Roman missionaries pushed northwards and came across the Christians of Northumbria, they were appalled at the unorthodox Christian practices they encountered.

This triggered off the controversy over tonsure and the celebration of Easter – both Churches holding deeply differentiated views over the two

▲ *Black rats – carriers of the plague or 'Black Death'*

subjects – which, at times, assumed all the bitterness of sectarian hatred. Oswy, a deeply religious man, belonged to the Celtic faith, whereas his wife Eanflaed of Mercia, was a devout adherent of the Roman Church. For some time, therefore, the Northumbrian court celebrated both Easters, a week apart. This intolerable situation was resolved at Whitby, when the Roman delegates won the day. The decision to go with the Roman Church over Irish monasteries changed not only Northumbria, but also Scotland.

The Celtic monks immediately withdrew to Iona and were replaced by Roman priests. Matters were made worse by a split at Iona: with some monks accepting Roman rule and others clinging to their dying faith. The collapse of the Columban Church, which had done so much to bring Christianity to Scotland, was hastened in the eighth century by Norse attacks.

▲ *The Synod of Whitby*

The Peoples of Scotland

BETWEEN THE departure of the Romans in 401 and the unification of Scotland in 1034 the country was torn apart by struggles between people of four different races, as well as tribal dissension. The unreliable and fragmentary nature of Irish annals and Norse sagas provide little more than a vague picture, but the broad picture is reasonably clear.

Pictish stone at Aberlemno ▼

BY THE TIME of the arrival of Columba, with his followers, in 563, the northern part of Britain was still largely dominated by the Picts, of whom the chief tribal groups were the Caledonii occupying the Grampians, the Highlands and the Islands, and the

Maeatae in Kincardineshire, Fife and Perthshire. Despite this, little of the Picts has survived, other than a number of ornately carved and incised stone slabs and a handful of placenames. Of all the peoples of Scotland, they have left the barest legacy, other than their blood which courses in the veins of many Scots to this day.

Two small states – although one can hardly call them that – were Manaan and Calatria. The first, about the upper reaches of the Forth, gives its name to such places as Clackmannan and Slamannan, and was based on Stirling which, down the centuries, has been the key to Scotland, north and south, and was therefore constantly fought over by its larger and more powerful neighbours. Calatria, roughly equivalent to today's West Lothian, was a buffer between the southern Picts, the Angles of Lothian and the Britons of Strathclyde.

In the far north elements of the original pre-Celtic Picts may have survived, but else-where the Picts had changed and now spoke Goidelic (Q-Celtic), and had much more in common with the Celts of Ireland than with those in the more northern areas of the land.

▲ *Pictish cross at Aberlemno*

The Britons of Strathclyde

THE SOUTH-WEST of Scotland (the area that is modern Renfrewshire, parts of Dunbartonshire, Lanarkshire, Ayrshire and Dumfriesshire) formed the kingdom of Strathclyde, taking its name from the valley of the Clyde.

IT WAS OCCUPIED by Brythonic (P–Celtic) peoples. Displaced by the invasions of the Angles, Saxons and Jutes in Roman Britain, the Britons had settled in those parts of the island where Roman rule had scarcely penetrated, from Cornwall to Cumbria, and Strathclyde was a northerly extension of this. Had these Brythonic peoples believed in a common cause, they might have withstood Anglo–Saxon pressure, but instead they were riven by internal quarrels. As a result of the battle of Arderydd (perhaps Arthuret near Carlisle) in 573, they split into two, and thereafter Strathclyde was a separate entity, with its capital at Alcluyd (Dumbarton).

Later attempts to reunify the Britons were finally thwarted by Aethelfrith of Northumbria, who defeated them at Chester in 613. The most civilised (in relative terms) of the races in north Britain, the Strathclyde Britons gradually lost ground to their more warlike neighbours.

Ultimately they would be absorbed by their Anglian rivals, their distinctive language recalled only in the numerous Welsh-sounding placenames of the south-west.

Galloway (modern Wigtownshire and Kirkcudbrightshire) was inhabited by an ancient Celtic race, sometimes known as the Gallovidians or Galloway Picts, but apparently quite separate. This remote, mountainous district continued as a more or less separate entity till the fourteenth century.

▲ *Dumbarton Castle*

The Scots of Dalriada

ACCORDING TO THE Irish annals, three sons of Erc, King of Dalriada in northern Ireland, crossed the sea between 498 and 503 and founded a new Dalriada in what is now Argyll and the Inner Hebrides.

THE NAME of this people, also known as a warlike people, first appears in Roman records about 400 as 'Scotti', to denote a tribe of Hiberni, and it is clear that, even by that date, they were harrying the northwestern coasts of Roman Britain. (The name 'Scots' is believed to be a corrupted form of Scotti or Scottus, which meant 'raiders'.) A century later they arrived as colonists and settled in Kintyre, fixing their capital at Dunadd. They were Goidelic-speaking Celts, Christianised by Patrick. They were a Celtic, warrior, combative and expansive race.

From the sons of Erc came four petty kingdoms which fought each other. Not until the advent of Columba did the Scots of Dalriada resolve their differences. Under the banner of Columban Christianity they began to make some headway against the Picts. At the Synod of Drumsceatt (near modern Derry) in 575, Columba used all his diplomatic skills to win recognition for Aidan of Dalriada as a ruler independent of Ireland. Aidan was an able ruler who secured peace with the Picts and helped the Britons to withstand the incursion of the Angles.

Decisively defeated by the Angles in 603 and 642, the Scots descended into tribal chaos once more. Weakened by internal strife, they were eventually subdued in 736 by Angus MacFergus of the Picts. Allied to

Mercia, Angus even made war on Northumbria and then, in 756, leagued with Northumbria, he attacked Strathclyde. By the time of his death in 761 he was effective ruler of Dalriada and Strathclyde as well as Pictland.

▲ *The site of Dunnad Hill-fort*

The Angles of Bernicia

TEUTONIC PIRATES from Frisia had been raiding the south-east coast of Scotland since the early fifth century. In 547, Ida, chief of the Angles, carved out a kingdom known as Bernicia which eventually extended from the Forth to the Tees. With the subordinate kingdom of Deira, Bernicia made up the territory known today as Northumbria.

EARLY IN THE seventh century Northumbria was one of the most powerful states in all Britain. Edwin, who reigned till 631, fortified the rock known as Edwinesburh and thus laid the foundations for Scotland's capital. Despite many setbacks, including defeats by Mercia, Northumbria rose again under Oswald, who reunited Bernicia and Deira and for a time dominated Pictland, Strathclyde and Dalriada.

By his decisive victory at Maserfield in 642, Penda of Mercia destroyed Northumbrian hegemony in north Britain for more than a decade, however under Oswiu its fortunes were restored. Defeating Penda at Winwaed near Leeds in 655, he made Northumbria stronger than ever, though his greatest legacy was to bring north Britain within the orbit of Rome.

This reign marks the zenith of Northumbria, a kingdom that now extended from the Forth to the Humber and (in Scotland) occupied the modern counties of the Borders and the Lothians. Out of the Teutonic language of the Angles would develop that form of Northern English which would eventually be spoken all over the Lowlands of Scotland.

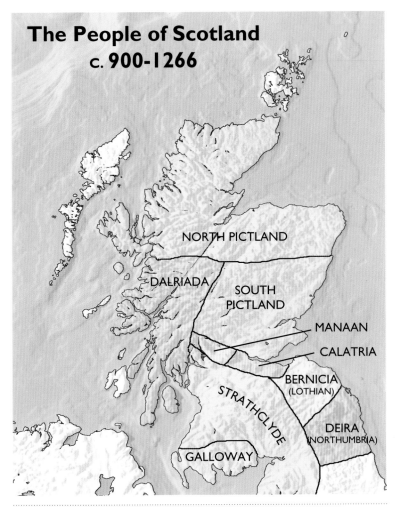

The People of Scotland
c. 900-1266

NORTH PICTLAND

DALRIADA

SOUTH PICTLAND

MANAAN

CALATRIA

BERNICIA
(LOTHIAN)

STRATHCLYDE

DEIRA
(NORTHUMBRIA)

GALLOWAY

▲ *Map of Scotland c. 900–1266*

Nectansmere, 685

NORTHUMBRIA might have become the core of a unified North Britain, but after Oswiu's death in 670 it went into decline.

O SWIU'S SUCCESSOR Ecgfrith was confronted by internal dissension as well as by a concerted attack by the Picts in 671. Though this invasion was repulsed, the Picts remained a constant threat. Eventually, in 685, Ecgfrith organised a great expedition and advanced into southern Pictland. At Nectansmere (Dunnichen in Angus) the Pictish army under Brude clashed with the Northumbrians. Ecgfrith was killed and his troops massacred, thus putting an end to any further Northumbrian (Angle) northward expansion.

It was a disaster from which Northumbria never recovered. Not only did the Picts free themselves from the shackles of the Angles, but the Scots of Dalriada and the Britons of Strathclyde regained their independence.

Thereafter, Northumbria no longer played a key role in the shaping of the country north of the Tweed and the centre of power shifted back to the land of the Picts.

In one respect, however, the influence of Northumbria continued to be felt. Brude's successor, Nectan, finally made the break with the Celtic Church in 710. Seven years later Iona followed suit and, as a result, Dalriada embraced the Roman faith. Only Strathclyde held out, and continued for some years longer to adhere to the Celtic Church.

The Picts were the dominant race in the eighth century. Constantine I, who succeeded Angus MacFergus in 789, consolidated the gains made by his father. Had the battle at Nectansmere never happened, a nation known as Scotland might never have existed.

▲ *Pictish carvings*

Norse Invasions

IN 793, THE FIRST descent on the Northumbrian coast by the Vikings (plunderers from Norway) took place. These raids, which increased in frequency and intensity over the ensuing years, weakened and eventually destroyed Northumbria. No longer would the Anglian kingdom play a dominant role in the affairs of either Scotland or England.

THE PICTS AND SCOTS were given no chance to profit from the misfortunes of Northumbria. In 794, attracted by the wealth of the monasteries, the Norsemen arrived and raided the Hebrides. In 802, they sacked the sacred monastery at Iona itself. From 795 onwards they raided Ireland and eventually settled there. By the middle of the ninth century they had established a Hiberno-Norse empire that stretched from Shetland and Orkney to the Isle of Man, and encompassed all the western islands of Scotland as well as much of Ireland.

THE VIKING'S SHIP.

▲ *Illustration of a Viking ship, and details of its features*

The Norsemen raided Iona a second time (806), and the entire Iona community was murdered and the buildings plundered. The monks of St Ninian's island, Shetland, were also attacked. After this, Constantine moved the ecclesiastical centre to Dunkeld. *Lia fail*, the Stone of Destiny which tradition regarded as the very pillow on which Jacob had dreamed of heaven, and which for centuries had been used in the crowning of Scottish, Pictish and Irish kings, was transferred to Scone. These moves, born out of necessity, paved the way towards the union of the Picts and the Scots.

Constantine, who died in 820, did not himself live long enough to see this accomplished. The annals are silent on the events of the ensuing quarter of a century, and the manner in which the Scots and Picts were united is conjectural.

▲ *Orkney farmland today*

Kenneth MacAlpin

PICTISH SOCIETY was matriarchal, and the crown passed by maternal descent. In this manner it appears that Kenneth, son of Alpin, King of Dalriada, claimed the Pictish throne through his mother, a Pictish princess.

KENNETH became ruler of Dalriada in 841, three years before he made his bid for the Pictish crown. The annals provide no satisfactory clues as to how the ruler of the relatively insignificant Scottish kingdom succeeded in taking over his larger and more powerful neighbour. History would repeat itself in 1603, and the reasons in 844 were probably not dissimilar. For several generations the Picts and Scots had been coming closer together, their ruling houses linked by marriage.

A clue is provided by the Huntingdon chronicle which stated that Danish pirates had made serious incursions into the Pictish mainland and slaughtered the inhabitants. Taking advantage of the Picts reeling under Norse attack, Kenneth

◀ *Cross on Islay*

led his army into Pictland. Apart from a vague reference to him slaying many Picts and driving out the others, we know of no decisive battle in this campaign, and it seems likely that Kenneth's claim to the Pictish throne was accepted without much opposition. Kenneth is said to have murdered seven earls – kinsmen who might have disputed his claim to the throne – all of which is reputed to have taken place during a celebration banquet at Scone.

He established his capital at Forteviot in Perthshire, in the very heart of Pictland, but it was from the incomers that the united kingdom of the Picts and Scots would eventually take its name. The monkish chronicles refer to it as Albania, the Latin form of the Gaelic Alba or Albainn which, in turn, would be anglicised as Albany, the ducal title of the eldest son of Scottish kings in the fifteenth century.

▲ *Danish pirates attacked the Pictish mainland*

The Emergence of Scotland, 844–1034

KENNETH MACALPIN died of cancer in 858 and was interred among his ancestors at Iona. The consolidation of his kingdom would take 190 years, and of the 15 kings that followed him two-thirds would meet a violent end, on the battlefield or from an assassin's dagger.

WHAT IS REMARKABLE is that the Picts, who must have been the dominant factor in the merger, now vanish from the scene. Kenneth's successors might be styled the kings of Picts and Scots, but Pictish identity ceases from 844 onwards. Some of the trouble facing successive rulers came from within as well as from the Britons of Strathclyde, the Angles of Lothian or the Norsemen. On one occasion the Britons sacked

▼ *Brechin Round Tower: Scots' architecture in Pictland*

Dunblane; on another the Danes pillaged Dunkeld. Kenneth himself made several attempts to subjugate Lothian, as the land between the Forth and Tweed was now known.

Having the same title as his father, Constantine II (863–77), son of Kenneth, was hard-pressed by the Norsemen, who showed no fear of dying during combat – it was their means of entering Vahala, the great warriors' reward in Asgaard. Olaf the White, King of Dublin, invaded Strathclyde in 866 and again in 870 when Dumbarton fell to the enemy. A permanent Danish settlement on the Solway is recalled to this day in such placenames as Lockerbie, Sibbaldbie and Middlebie. Olaf's son Thorstein invaded the far north in 875 and overran much of northern Pictland. In 890, Harald Harfagr, ruler of Norway, seized the Orkney and Western Isles and installed jarls or earls. From Rognvald, first Jarl of Orkney, was descended Rollo who conquered Normandy and was the ancestor of William the Conqueror.

▲ *Viking raiders in the North Sea*

The Battle of Brunanburh, 934

OF THE LATER rulers, the most successful was Constantine III (900–42) whose long reign was a period of consolidation after he decisively defeated the Hiberno-Norse in 903.

EARLY IN THIS reign, the royal line of Strathclyde died out and Constantine's brother Donald was elected King. However, dynastic union did not bring peace between Strathclyde and the Scots, but a century later it would result in the absorption of the British kingdom into Scotland.

▲ *Bamburgh Castle, the reputed site of battle*

In 918, Constantine joined forces with Eldred of Lothian in combatting a renewed attack by the Danes of Ireland. There was an inconclusive battle in which Constantine and Eldred were defeated but the Danes were too weak to follow up their success. Constantine bought peace by marrying his daughter to Olaf Sihtricsson, King of Dublin, but this alliance brought him into conflict with Aethelstan of Wessex, the most powerful king in England.

In 934, Aethelstan invaded Alba and forced Constantine to sue for peace, but three years later the Scots, Britons and Danes combined to attack Aethelstan at Brunanburh (Burnswark in Dumfriesshire). The allies were soundly defeated and Constantine forced to submit once more. After Aethelstan's death Constantine handed over his throne to his cousin Malcolm and retired to a monastery.

Malcolm I (942–54) waged war in Moray and Lothian. In the reign of his successor Indulph (954–62), Edinburgh fell into Scottish hands for all time.

▲ *Viking silver lion*

Carham

UNDER KENNETH II (971–95) Lothian fell to the Scots. The kingdom of Northumbria had disintegrated in 966, the southern part (Deira) coming under English rule. Edgar of England is said to have granted Lothian to Kenneth in exchange for some sort of acknowledgment of Edgar as his superior. This formed part of the argument, centuries later, that Scotland was a feudal dependency of England, but it rests on very doubtful authority.

I N 1005, KENNETH'S son Malcolm II became king. He began in fine style by invading Lothian, where Scottish rule had been purely nominal, and penetrated as far south as Durham, where he was defeated so severely that for 12 years he left Lothian alone. Instead he turned his attention northwards. Sigurd of Orkney had defeated the Mormaer of Moray and strengthened his hold on Caithness and Sutherland. By diplomacy rather than force of arms, Malcolm secured an alliance with Sigurd, giving him his daughter in marriage.

Rejoicing following the battle of Clontarf ▶

When Sigurd was killed at the battle of Clontarf in Ireland in 1014, Malcolm made Thorfinn, Sigurd's son and his own grandson, Earl of Caithness and Sutherland, and thereby ensured his loyalty. Having secured his northern and western frontiers, Malcolm addressed himself to the problem of Lothian. In 1018, he led his army into battle against an Angle army from Northumbria at Carham on Tweed, and brought the rich Lothians under Malcolm II's rule. Henceforward all the land north of the Tweed would be recognised as the dominion of the Scots; Scotland and her borders were now stable, though not necessarily for long. King Canute confirmed the cession of Lothian, but 16 years elapsed before it was actually accomplished.

▲ *King Canute*

The Conquest of Lothian, 1018-34

BY THE CESSION of 1018, Malcolm II became nominal ruler of the land between the Tweed and the Pentland Firth, but almost 250 years would elapse before Scotland emerged in something like its present form.

IN 1018, OWEN, the last King of Strathclyde, died. Malcolm engineered the succession of his grandson Duncan, in the hope that in the fullness of time Duncan would, of course, succeed to the whole of Scotland. Thereafter, Strathclyde was effectively a dependency of the Scottish crown.

The rest of Malcolm's reign was taken up largely in subduing revolts in Moray (always a troublesome area), as well as consolidating his position in Lothian. In connection with the latter, he seems to have fallen foul of Canute, who had been eyeing Scotland for a long time, especially the Lothian area, which he considered to be his by right. Canute (also known as 'Cnut' or 'Knut') invaded Scotland in 1031 and wrung some sort of an admission of feudal superiority out of Malcolm.

More importantly, the ancient law of tanistry, by which a system of alternate succession had ensured the leap-frogging of rulers from two closely related families, was abandoned in favour of the newfangled concept of primogeniture. Malcolm is said to have settled the matter by having the heir apparent from the house of Kenneth eliminated in the customary brutal fashion.

The following year (1034), Malcolm died. His obituary described him as King of Scotia, the first time that this term had been applied to Scotland rather than that portion of Ireland whence came the Dalriadic Scots. He was succeeded, as he wished, by his grandson Duncan, son of Crinan, abbot of Dunkeld.

◄ *King Canute*

Development of English Influence

DUNCAN (who was not the ageing and venerable monarch portrayed by William Shakespeare in *Macbeth*) was the first king to rule over the land of the Picts and Scots, Lothian and Strathclyde, giving real meaning to the name of Scotia. The frontiers of the Scottish kingdom were still further extended, reaching far down into what is now English territory. His reign, however, beginning in 1034, turned out to be more nominal than real.

H E HAD NO SOONER entered on his inheritance than he was attacked by Aldred, Earl of Northumbria, who plundered Strathclyde. Whether prior to this attack, or because of it, Duncan led an expedition into England and besieged Durham with disastrous results. In turn, this seems to have encouraged Earl Thorfinn of Caithness to rebel. Having ousted his half-brothers from Orkney, Thorfinn repulsed all attempts by Duncan, including the deployment of the Scottish fleet. At Torfness (probably

▲ *Duncan I*

Burghead) Thorfinn defeated Duncan and advanced as far as Fife.

Duncan's inept handling of Thorfinn seems to have disgusted the Mormaer of Moray, Macbeth. His wife, Gruoch, was a granddaughter of Kenneth III and under the law of tanistry this gave him a strong claim to the throne. In 1040, Macbeth killed Duncan at Bothgouanan near Elgin and seized the throne.

Macbeth made the mistake of allowing Duncan's elder son Malcolm Canmore ('big chief') to escape to England, where he was raised by his maternal uncle, Earl Siward of Northumbria. The younger son, Donald Bane, was packed off to relatives in the Western Isles, where he was brought up in a Hiberno-Norse tradition that would be very different from the English upbringing of his elder brother, and a source of dissension between them in later years.

▲ *William Shakespeare and contemporaries*

Macbeth, 1040-57

FEW RULERS have had such a bad press as Macbeth, thanks to Shakespeare. In fact, he seems to have been an able and wise king, as his reign of 17 years testifies. Under his reign, the people of north and south Scotland were united and a stable Scottish kingdom looked likely.

APART FROM AN ABORTIVE counter-coup led by Crinan, father of the murdered Duncan, Macbeth's reign was relatively free of trouble. His throne was secure enough for him to make a pilgrimage to Rome in 1050. He organised troops of men to patrol the wilder countryside in an attempt to enforce some kind of law and order. He also made generous grants of land and privileges, not only to the established Church but also to the Culdees or Keledei (literally 'companions of God'), an ascetic sect which had arisen among the Picts and flourished for 200 years, with important centres at Lochleven, Scone, Dunkeld ('fort of the Culdees'), St Andrews and other places in Fife and Perthshire.

In 1054, Siward of Northumbria invaded Scotland, possibly with the intention of setting Malcolm Canmore on his father's throne. Significantly, there was no uprising in support of the invasion, as one might have expected had Macbeth's regime been unpopular. Instead, the Scots rallied to their king and beat back the invader.

Three years later, however, Malcolm himself invaded Scotland. His wife was Ingibjorg, daughter of Earl Thorfinn of Orkney, a powerful ally in his struggle to wrest the throne from Macbeth. Nothing is recorded about the campaign itself, other than that Macbeth and Malcolm clashed at Lumphanan in Aberdeenshire, and that Macbeth the usurper was killed.

▲ *A scene from Shakespeare's* Macbeth

Malcolm III Canmore, 1057-93

WITH THE SUPPORT of the Earls of Orkney and Northumbria, and the backing of the Church in respect of his descent from Crinan of Dunkeld, Malcolm III Canmore ('big' or 'great' 'chief') had little difficulty in securing the throne, although he was not always a consistent ruler.

WITH MALCOLM on the throne, Scotland would have the 'English Party' forever, ingrained in Lowland beliefs and politics. The only opposition came from Moray, where Macbeth's son Lulach had become Mormaer or governor, but within months Malcolm had crushed the revolt at Strathbogie and Lulach was killed in battle. In 1061, Malcolm turned his attention to Northumbria where he took advantage of the absence of the new Earl, Tostig, on pilgrimage to Rome, to plunder at will.

During the momentous year of 1066, Malcolm watched the rapid turn of events which brought Harold

◀ *Malcolm III*

Godwinesson to the English throne, the revolt of Earl Tostig and his defeat at Stamford Bridge, and the invasion of Duke William of Normandy. During the years of his exile, Malcolm had spent some time at the court of Edward the Confessor, and in support of the brother of his second wife Margaret he embarked on an invasion of England in 1070.

The expedition was launched from Cumbria, then still the southern province of Strathclyde, and advanced east to overrun the area between the Tees and Tyne. While doing so, Malcolm was attacked from the rear by Earl Cospatric of Northumbria, hitherto a staunch ally. In 1072, William the Conqueror came north with an army and ran Malcolm to earth at Abernethy, where Malcolm 'became William's man', an act of homage that would lay up much trouble for the Scots centuries later.

Malcolm again raided Northumbria in 1079. When the Normans retaliated in 1080 by penetrating Scotland as far as the Carron, the Scots melted before them, a tactic they used effectively many times in later years.

▲ *Edward the Confessor*

Queen Margaret

THE ENGLISH influence on Scotland, begun by isolated acts of submission from Scottish landowners, was considerably rein-forced by the advent of Queen Margaret, an Anglo-Saxon princess whom Malcolm took as his second wife.

THE LAST OF THE OLD Anglo-Saxon royal line, Edgar the Atheling, with his sisters Margaret and Christina, fled to Scotland after the Norman Conquest and were given sanctuary. (Most of the Anglo-Saxon nobility fled to the Lowlands of Scotland as a safe haven from the Norman invaders.)

▲ *Edward the Confessor*

Malcolm's wife Ingibjorg had died leaving three young sons, so he married Margaret, a saintly and very determined young woman, in 1069. Though born in Hungary, Margaret had been raised at the court of Edward the Confessor. Her piety and cultivated manners had a civilising influence on her husband.

Margaret's father was the great-nephew of Edward the Confessor, while her maternal grandfather was St Stephen of Hungary. Though half her husband's age she wielded enormous power over him. She introduced Continental fashions and manners, and transformed the Scottish court. Foreign merchants were encouraged to trade with Scotland and in their wake came new industries and technology.

Margaret's greatest impact was in the religious field. Though nominally Christian, Scotland was very haphazard in its religious observance. Singlehandedly, she strove to reform abuses in worship and ritual. She rebuilt Iona, endowed churches and religious houses, notably the great abbey at Dunfermline, and was lavish in her charity to the poor. Her chapel in Edinburgh Castle is one of the oldest extant buildings in Scotland, while North and South Queensferry are a reminder of the service she instituted for the benefit of pilgrims to and from St Andrews.

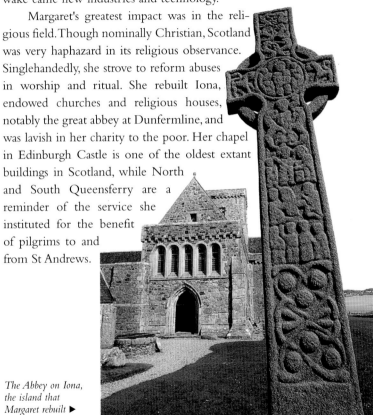

The Abbey on Iona, the island that Margaret rebuilt ▶

English Clergy and Court

QUEEN MARGARET was canonised in 1251 in recognition of her saintly life. Unlike her kinswoman and contemporary, St Elizabeth, she never had the opportunity to retire to the contemplative life of the convent, but made it her life's work to reclaim the people of her adopted land from their ignorant ways.

◀ St Margaret

ALTHOUGH SHE accomplished much in the erection of abbeys and churches, in other ecclesiastical matters Margaret could do little more than lay the foundations on which her sons could build.

One of her greatest ambitions was to reorganise the Scottish Church on orthodox Roman lines. She could not introduce the diocesan system until Scotland's one and only bishopric, at St Andrews, fell vacant, and this did not happen till after her death. She was powerless to reform the monastic system because Malcolm and his nobles (deriving much of their revenue from the monasteries) had a vested interest in keeping things as they were.

Due directly to Margaret's influences, Scottish court life assumed an English tinge, while in the church a system of regular diocesan episcopacy gradually took shape. She recruited priests from England to set a good example to the wayward Scots and she lavished money on the Culdees, whom she regarded as a shining example of the pure religious spirit.

Her family and retainers formed the nucleus of an English-speaking court. Anglo-Saxon refugees and later Normans were invited to a court whose dress and ceremonial aped that of the English and Continental monarchies. Margaret bore Malcolm six sons, and every one of them was given the name of an English king. By the time of Margaret's death in 1093 the Scottish court and clergy had been radically transformed.

▼ *St Margaret's Chapel*

Anglicisation of the Scottish Church

MALCOLM III and his eldest son Edward were killed in 1093 while raiding in Northumbria. The dying Margaret expired when her third son Edgar brought the tragic news, piously uttering a prayer of thanks that '...such sadness should have been sent, to purify my final moments'. Malcolm's remains were laid to rest alongside his wife, in Dunfermline Abbey, 20 years later.

MARGARET undoubtedly wore herself out in her heroic efforts to reform the Scottish church. On one occasion she argued for three whole days against the representatives of the Scottish clergy before winning the argument. She persuaded the Scots to fall into line regarding the beginning of Lent, the reception of the Eucharist on Easter Day, the Roman celebration of the Mass, a stricter observance of Sunday and the suppression of marriage within certain prohibited degrees.

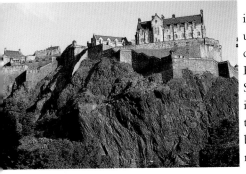

The clergy bowed to the inevitable, but among the population at large there was disquiet at the number of English settlers moving into Scotland and acquiring land. It is significant that, on news of the death of Malcolm, his brother Donald Bane raised a rebellion and besieged

▲ *Edinburgh Castle, besieged by Donald Bane*

Edinburgh Castle from which Margaret's sons barely escaped with their mother's corpse. Antipathy to the late Queen was so strong that her sons had to flee the country.

The English were expelled and the Celtic nature of Scotland was rapidly reasserted, but Donald Bane was himself ousted six months later. Ironically the challenge came from Duncan, Malcolm's eldest son by Ingibjorg. Surrendered to William the Conqueror as a hostage, he had lived at the Norman court since 1072. Supported by William Rufus, to whom he had sworn fealty, Duncan invaded Scotland in 1094 with an Anglo-Norman army and defeated Donald Bane.

▲ *William the Conqueror*

Anglicisation of the Administrative System

DUNCAN was overthrown within months, slain in battle at Mondynes, Kincardineshire by a combination of Donald Bane and Edmund, son of Margaret and Malcolm III.

FOR 30 YEARS following Margaret's death, Scotland was in turmoil, ruled over by a sucession of insecure, weak kings. As a result, the Normans found themselves with increasing power, and began to take lands in lowland Scotland as they did in Ireland. Scotland was partitioned, with Donald Bane ruling the Celtic north and Edmund the south. This situation, which turned the clock back to the time of Kenneth MacAlpin, lasted till 1097. It was overturned by Margaret's brother, Edgar the Atheling, who had been living at the Norman court. With an Anglo-Norman army provided by the ever-obliging Rufus, he invaded Scotland, banished both usurpers and installed his nephew and namesake as King.

Edgar (1097–1107) was very much his mother's son and lost no time in carrying on where she had left off. Although it is too early to speak of a settled Scottish capital, it was significant that Edgar preferred Edinburgh to Dunfermline, which had been his father's favourite residence. Although styled King of Scots, he addressed his subjects in his charters as Scots and English. More importantly, the names of the witnesses to his charters were almost entirely English.

Edgar relied heavily on the support of William Rufus, but he paid dearly for this by openly acknowledging Rufus as his liege lord. His ties with England were strengthened by the marriage of his sister Eadgyth to

Henry I; she abandoned her Anglo-Saxon name in favour of Matilda or Maud. This marriage with a princess of the old Anglo-Saxon line also strengthened Henry's hold over his English subjects.

▲ *Church of the Knights Templar – the architecture shows English influence*

Introduction of the Feudal System

BEFORE HIS DEATH in 1107, Edgar arranged that his brother Alexander should succeed him as King of Scots, but ruling over Edinburgh and the land north of the Forth-Clyde isthmus. The rest (Lothian and Strathclyde) would be governed by his youngest brother David as Earl.

THE REASONS FOR this decision were twofold. Edgar realised the difficulty of governing the Celtic Highlands and increasingly anglicised Lowlands as a single entity. He also wished to make a distinction between an area over which the King had sole sovereignty, and an area which, it could be argued, was held as a fief of the English King.

Alexander I (1107–24) married the English King Henry I's daughter, Sibylla, while his sister married the English King himself. Alexander

acquired his epithet of 'the Fierce' from the ruthless suppression of a Celtic revolt in Moray and the Mearns. Shortly afterwards he founded an Augustinian monastery at Scone and staffed it with English clerics. He also established monasteries in Moray, using the Church as an effective

▲ *Bothwell, feudal castle*

▲ *Dirleton, feudal castle*

way of curbing rebelliousness. At the same time he suppressed the Culdees, who represented the old Celtic language and way of life.

David spent several years at the court of his sister and brother-in-law, who made him Earl of Northampton. He married the heiress of two other English earldoms, Huntingdon and Northumbria, and thus became one of the greatest magnates in England. In Lothian and Strathclyde he pursued an Anglo-Norman policy, introducing the feudal system of land tenure, and making generous grants of land to his Anglo-Norman barons. Existing landholders were not dispossessed; they merely held their rights from their new lord, rather than from the crown direct.

David I, 1124–53

HAD THE DIVISION of Scotland between the brothers continued, Lothian and Strathclyde might have become part of England. The death of Alexander in 1124 without issue, however, meant that David succeeded to the throne and thus reunited the Highlands and Lowlands.

DAVID I HAD RECEIVED a Norman education and grew to love Norman and Anglo-Saxon culture. As well as reuniting the Highlands and Lowlands, he granted charters to many landlords – many of whom were his Anglo-Saxon friends – who were glad to exchange the uncertainties of tribal tenure for written guarantees of their rights and privileges. Gradually the feudal system was extended to the whole country. The great landowners, both the Anglo-Norman incomers and the old Scottish nobility, intermarried.

The diocese of St Andrews had been vacant since the death of the last Celtic bishop, Modach, in 1093; but in 1108 Alexander had appointed his late mother's confessor and biographer, Turgot, as bishop. When Turgot regarded the Archbishop of York as his superior, Alexander replaced him with Eadmer from Canterbury who naturally insisted that his archbishop should be recognised as primate of all Britain. Not till the death of

Eadmer in 1124 was the bishopric filled by a cleric to the King's liking, Robert, Prior of Scone.

Bishoprics were created by Alexander in Moray and Dunkeld, and this policy was endorsed by David who created all the medieval dioceses of Scotland by the end of his reign. His lavish endowment of the Church and building of cathedrals, abbeys and churches earned him the epithet of *sair sanct* (sore saint) for the crown. Thus the Church, like the nobility, became the instrument for the anglicisation of Scotland.

▲ *Scone Abbey, home of Robert, Prior of Scone*

The Battle of the Standard, 1138

DESPITE THE anglicisation of Scotland, relations between David I and England were not always cordial. The border was ill-defined, and David had ambitions to annex Cumbria (which historically had been part of Strathclyde) as well as Northumbria (of whose earldom his wife was heiress).

AS EARL OF Northampton, David had signed the bond of 1127 promising his fealty to Henry's daughter Matilda. When Henry I died in 1135, and the English throne was seized by Stephen of Blois, David invaded the northern counties of England in support of his niece Matilda. In 1136 his troops seized every castle in Cumberland and Northumberland (except Bamborough) and advanced as far as Durham. Stephen came north and hammered out a deal whereby David gave up his conquests in exchange for the grant of the earldom of Huntingdon to his son Henry and the promise that his claim to the earldom of Northumberland would be considered.

This peace lasted only a few months. On the pretext of an insult to his son Henry by the Archbishop of Canterbury, David broke off diplomatic relations. In 1138 he invaded England and was defeated near Northallerton at the Battle of the Standard (so called on account of the ship's mast bearing the banners of English saints), but Stephen, now embroiled in civil war with Matilda's followers, was unable to exploit the situation.

Stephen granted Northumberland as an English fief to David's heir, Henry. This generous act did not secure peace. When Matilda's son (the

Durham, the extent of David's advance into England ▶

future Henry II) made his bid for the throne in 1149, David backed him in return for a promise of all the land north of the Tyne.

Malcolm the Maiden, 1153–65

DAVID I died in 1153, and as his son Henry had predeceased him, the Scottish throne passed to his 12-year-old grandson, who reigned as Malcolm IV – however he is best remembered as 'the Maiden' on account of his effeminate appearance.

THE ANGLICISATION of Scotland still had a long way to go, as events early in this reign proved. On Malcolm's accession, Donald MacHeth raised a revolt in Moray, aided by Somerled of Argyll, and for three years waged war in many parts of the country.

Although Malcolm eventually put down this rebellion he was less successful in his dealings with England. He was surrounded by Norman advisors, and this, in itself, caused many problems. In 1154, Stephen died and was succeeded by Matilda's son as Henry II. He proved to be an energetic and capable monarch, and having restored law and order in his own realm he turned his attentions to Scotland.

In 1157, Henry and Malcolm met at Chester. Advised by his magnates

▲ *Kilmartin Stones, which date back to Malcolm's time*

(who were all considerable landholders in England as well as Scotland), Malcolm was induced to surrender all the territorial gains made by his grandfather. As a sop, he was allowed to retain the Honour of Huntingdon. In 1159, he won his spurs fighting in the English expedition against Toulouse.

He was still in France when he heard that a Celtic revolt had broken out. Hurrying back to Scotland, he came to terms with the rebels at Perth (1160), but no sooner had he dealt with this matter than he faced rebellion in Galloway. At the third attempt he suppressed this uprising, only to be faced with an invasion of Renfrewshire by Somerled, backed by an army from Ireland and the Hebrides. The mysterious deaths of Somerled and his sons (1164) nipped this danger in the bud.

▲ *Henry II*

The Treaty of Falaise, 1174

MALCOLM died at Jedburgh in 1165 and was succeeded by his brother William, known as 'the Lion' on account of his martial prowess (the red lion rampant on a yellow field were to become Scotland's heraldic colours, the Royal Standard), though it did not always stand him in good stead.

AT FIRST HE WAS on good terms with Henry II and accompanied him on his campaigns in France, for which he received the Honour of Huntingdon previously held by his brother. But William was determined to add Cumberland and Northumberland to his dominions (his predecessor, Malcolm IV, having returned Northumbria to England under the threat of invasion), and much of his long reign would be devoted to realising that ambition.

His opportunity came in 1174 when the son of Henry II, the future Henry III, conspired with him. In exchange for his help, Prince Henry promised William the whole of Northumberland, while William's brother David was promised the honours of Huntingdon and Cambridge. Consequently William invaded Northumberland and Cumberland,

▲ *William the Lion at Alnwick*

his undisciplined forces raping, pillaging and slaughtering at will. In July, however, a small but determined army organised by the barons of Yorkshire caught up with the Scots at Alnwick. In the confusion, William was captured and taken south. Henry II incarcerated him at Falaise in Normandy, and it was there, in December, that William agreed to a humiliating treaty.

He was forced to do homage for his entire kingdom, and to ensure that William behaved himself his brother David and 21 of the chief magnates of Scotland were to be held indefinitely as hostages, while the castles of Berwick, Edinburgh, Jedburgh, Roxburgh and Stirling were to be garrisoned by English troops.

▲ *Stirling Castle*

William the Lion, 1165-1214

EFFECTIVELY, by the treaty of Falaise, Scotland lost its independence. This situation continued until 1189 when Richard I cancelled the treaty and sold William back his crown in return for a large sum of money which Richard needed for the Third Crusade.

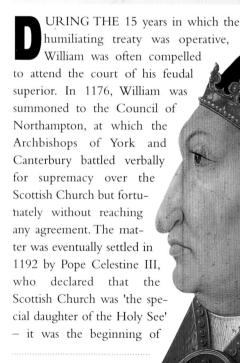

DURING THE 15 years in which the humiliating treaty was operative, William was often compelled to attend the court of his feudal superior. In 1176, William was summoned to the Council of Northampton, at which the Archbishops of York and Canterbury battled verbally for supremacy over the Scottish Church but fortunately without reaching any agreement. The matter was eventually settled in 1192 by Pope Celestine III, who declared that the Scottish Church was 'the special daughter of the Holy See' – it was the beginning of

Pope Alexander VI nullified Alexander III's interdict ▶

nearly 100 years of relative peace between England and Scotland. In the interim, William had been at loggerheads with Pope Alexander III, who went so far as to excommunicate him and place his kingdom under papal interdict in 1181. Alexander's death soon afterwards nullified these extreme measures. Scotland, however, had to wait until 1472 before St Andrews was made an archbishopric.

William never lost sight of his ambition to acquire Northumberland. In 1194 he even offered to buy it from the impecunious Richard, but Richard would only agree so long as its castles were not fortified. Later, he was prepared to let King John select a wife for his son and heir, a further admission of the English king as his feudal superior. This weakness towards England encouraged revolt in Scotland. Galloway (who had rebelled no less than three times against Malcolm IV), Moray, Ross and Caithness rebelled at various times up to 1212.

▲ *King John*

Alexander II, 1214-49

WILLIAM THE LION died at Stirling aged 73, the longest-reigning monarch in Scotland till the time of James VI (1567–1625). He was succeeded by his son Alexander, a boy of 16. Alexander was a capable ruler who put to good use the administrative machinery created by David I.

T HE REIGN BEGAN inauspiciously with yet another revolt in Moray, but it was speedily put down. Alexander inherited his father's ambition and seized the opportunity of the Barons' Revolt against King John to invade Northumberland, ostensibly as an ally of the barons. He invaded again in 1216 but was forced to come to terms with the new King, Henry III, and do homage at Berwick for his English fiefs, as well as formally renouncing his claims to the northern counties. In 1221, he married Henry's sister Joanna, and his own sister married Hubert de Burgh, the most powerful magnate in England.

When Hubert fell from grace in 1235 and Henry tried to reassert the claims in the treaty of

▲ *William the Lion*

Falaise, Alexander retaliated by renewing his own demands on the northern counties. This quarrel was patched up in 1236 when the two kings met at Newcastle. By the treaty of York, Alexander finally renounced his claims in exchange for estates in northern England.

Otherwise his time and energy were largely taken up in consolidating his kingdom and putting down Celtic revolts. In 1221–22, Alexander led expeditions against Argyll and pacified that unruly district with little bloodshed. In 1222 he punished the people of Caithness, who had roasted their unpopular bishop alive in his own kitchen. Another two revolts in Moray were promptly crushed, while campaigns in Galloway further reduced Celtic power.

Alexander II died in 1249 while on his way to attempt conquest of the Western Isles, whose lords still chose to give their allegiance to the kings of Norway.

▲ *Map of Scotland, England and Wales, mid-thirteenth century*

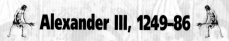

Alexander III, 1249–86

THE REIGNS OF ALEXANDER II and his son Alexander III are regarded as the golden age in Scotland's medieval history, a period in which anglicisation was largely completed, trade flourished, the burghs increased in size and importance, and roads and bridges improved communications.

ALEXANDER III WAS both the nephew and son-in-law of Henry III of England, marrying Henry's daughter Margaret in 1251, and thereby securing peace with England. Alexander was tactful and diplomatic and managed to maintain a distinct division between Scottish and English lands without riling the English king. Alexander also established cordial relations with his brother-in-law, later Edward I (known as the 'Hammer of the Scots'). During Alexander's reign, relations between Scotland and England were better than they had ever been, and Berwick, right on the border at the mouth of the Tweed, was the largest and most prosperous town in Scotland. The home trades improved, revenue increased, law and order were relatively well maintained, and education prospered. Life became less dangerous than it had been.

Although Scotland was at peace throughout this reign, it was never free from intrigue and conspiracy. Alexander was a boy of eight when he came to the throne and the leading magnates jostled for power. At first the rivalry was between the High Justiciar, Alan Durward, and the Comyn family, and this lasted till 1258 when the King came of age. Later power struggles involved Alexander the Steward of Scotland (progenitor of the

Stewart dynasty), the Earls of March and Strathearn, and, above all, the Lord of Annandale, Robert de Brus. In the underlying power play, Celt and Norman were often allied against others of the same ethnic groups, from which the later pro-English or Scottish parties would emerge.

▲ *King Edward I, Alexander's brother-in-law*

The Battle of Largs, 1263

HAVING PACIFIED the Scottish mainland, Alexander II turned his attention to the Hebrides. At first he offered to buy the islands from Haco of Norway and when this was rejected he organised an expedition but died at Kerrera, near Oban, in 1249, as his fleet was about to sail.

THUS IT FELL to his successor to advance this policy. In 1262 Alexander III sent a mission to Norway to negotiate the transfer of the offshore islands to Scotland. Haco not only spurned this overture but imprisoned the Scottish diplomats until pressured by Henry III to release them.

The following year, Haco brought his fleet to the Firth of Clyde, but after an inconsequential battle at Largs the remnants of the Norwegian fleet sailed off, having been defeated on land and at sea by the Scots; Haco died at Kirkwall on the homeward voyage, from injuries sustained in battle. The

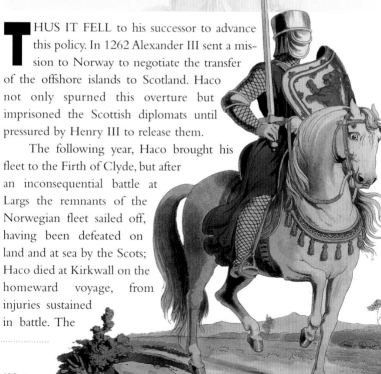

Isle of Man and the Western Isles submitted to Alexander soon afterwards, and in 1266 Eric, Haco's successor, formally ceded all of the Hebrides and Man to Scotland for a lump sum of 4,000 marks and a small annual payment. The treaty of 20 years before was sealed by the marriage of Eric and Alexander's daughter, Margaret. Centuries of war and strife was put to an end, and a friendly relationship ensued between the two countries, which has lasted to this day.

Although Orkney and Shetland remained in Norwegian or Danish hands till 1469, they were sufficiently remote not to pose the constant menace which the Hebrides had been. The removal of the Norse threat, however, completed the consolidation of the kingdom of Scotland.

Memorial commemorating the Battle of Largs ▶

◀ *Alexander II*

The Maid of Norway

POSTERITY would judge the reign of the last of the old line of Scottish kings as a golden age. The sudden and unfortunate death of Alexander III in March 1286 was the end of an era in more ways than one. It marked the end of the period of anglicisation and ushered in a realignment of Scotland with France against a common enemy, England.

ALEXANDER III was only 43 when he was killed in a riding accident near Kinghorn, Fife (he was not only thrown from his horse, but precipitated over a cliff). His first wife and all his children had predeceased him. His young bride, Joleta of Dreux, was at first thought to be pregnant, but this proved to be a false hope. Alexander's heir was, in fact, his infant granddaughter whose mother had married Eric of Norway and then died in 1283. Only a week after the death of Prince Alexander, the King's sole

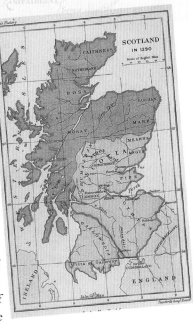

▲ *Map of Scotland in 1290*

surviving son, in 1284, Alexander III had summoned his council. There, 13 earls, 11 bishops and 25 barons had formally recognised Princess Margaret, the Maid of Norway, as heiress of Scotland, the Hebrides and the Isle of Man.

The intervention of Edward I of England was at first welcomed. He proposed a marriage between the Maid and his son (later Edward II). This amicable agreement anticipated the smooth, peaceful relations between the two countries, so arrangements were made to bring the Maid to Scotland. But in September 1290 fate dealt another blow: the Princess was taken ill on her way to England and she died in the Orkney Islands. Scotland was left with no heir to the throne.

▲ *Edward II*

Competition for the Throne

IT IS A MEASURE of the desperation of Alexander III and his council that the claims of a foreigner, a girl and a baby should have been accepted; but Alexander had no brother, nephew or cousin, nor was there any living legitimate descendant of any Scottish king later than David I.

THE THIRD OF HIS grandsons was David, Earl of Huntingdon, and from the descendants of his three daughters came the chief claimants to the Scottish throne. John Balliol was the grandson of the eldest daughter and by the law of primogeniture he should have got the throne. But this was as yet not clearly established, hence the counter-claim by Robert Bruce, son of the second daughter, who argued that he was closer to his grandfather, Earl David.

In fact, as far back as 1238, Alexander II (before the birth of the

◀ David I

future Alexander III) had recognised Bruce as his heir presumptive. Bruce had been quick to revive his claim when Alexander III died, but the council of Scottish magnates had decided that the minority of a baby queen was preferable to civil war between rival claimants.

As soon as the Maid's death became known, Bruce began raising an army and, at Perth, declared that the throne was his by right. On 7 October 1290, Bishop Fraser of St Andrews, one of the Guardians of Scotland, wrote to Edward I, urging him to intervene on behalf of John Balliol. Edward was already familiar with both the Balliol and Bruce families, and had misgivings about Robert Bruce's loyalty to England.

▲ *Robert Bruce's messenger visits the royal court*

Claims of English Overlordship

EDWARD I, in his self-proclaimed capacity as Superior and Lord Paramount of Scotland, summoned the Scottish barons and clergy to meet him at Norham-on-Tweed in May 1291. He gave them a few days to accept his new role, a decision aided by the presence of a large English army on the south bank of the Tweed. Many of the Scottish barons were Anglo-Norman, with estates in England as well as Scotland.

WHILE THE CASE of the rival claimants was being considered, Edward collected all available evidence in support of his own claim to feudal superiority over Scotland. A report on this was submitted to the English parliament on 2 June 1292 but its findings were inconclusive. When parliament met again, on 15 October, it concluded that if no law existed to settle the matter, it should be left to King Edward himself to decide the issue.

At Berwick on 17 November 1292, Edward declared in favour of John Balliol, who swore fealty to him the following day, at

◀ *Norham Castle, where Edward met the barons*

Edward's insistence. On 30 November, Balliol was crowned King at Scone and his feudal overlord made a grand progress as far as Perth. However, Balliol was humiliated and, despite many attempts to convince Scottish nobles that he had not given his loyalty over to the English, few believed him. The great seal used by the Guardians of Scotland was shattered, and the pieces deposited in the English Treasury. In this curious manner ended the Great Cause, in which the judge had a far greater vested interest than any of the contending parties.

▲ *Edward III, like his grandfather recaptured Berwick in 1333*

John Balliol, 1292-96

EDWARD soon made it clear that he regarded Balliol as his vassal. Whether he set out deliberately to humiliate Balliol is debatable, but he certainly treated him in an arrogant manner, involving him in lawsuits where he was compelled to answer before the English bar like any other subject.

WHEN BALLIOL tried to resist, Edward ordered him to surrender his chief castles, which henceforth were garrisoned by English troops. Their high-handed behaviour led to resistance among the Scots.

In 1295, Edward, already embroiled in domestic problems and a revolt in Wales, mounted an expedition to Gascony against France. Balliol, desperate to prove to his fellow Scots that he was not as weak-willed as they claimed him to be, negotiated a defensive agreement with the French, the beginning of the Auld Alliance, and invaded Cumberland in 1296. In revenge Edward besieged Berwick and massacred its inhabitants, killing women and children as well as the army. The Scottish army was soundly defeated at Dunbar, and the castles of Roxburgh, Edinburgh and Stirling capitulated.

Finally, on 7 July 1296, Balliol himself submitted to his overlord at Stracathro, surrendered his regalia, abdicated the throne and went into exile. Edward destroyed the Great

▲ *Edward I in battle*

Seal of Scotland, had the national archives shipped off to London and, the greatest insult of all, removed the Stone of Destiny from Scone and placed it in Westminster Abbey where it would remain for the next 700 years. In October, Edward, the 'Hammer of the Scots', returned to England, leaving Scotland under English military administration. After his campaign, Scotland was left a devastated mess.

◄ *Devorgilla Bridge, Dumfries, named after Balliol's wife*

William Wallace

JOHN DE WARENNE, Earl of Surrey, was appointed military governor, Hugh de Cressingham treasurer and William Ormsby justiciar. The Scottish barons, clergy and other leading figures swore allegiance to Edward and subscribed their names to the list known as Ragman's Roll.

EDWARD HAD RIDDEN home in the confidence that Scotland was now secured. He was wrong. From Warenne and Cressingham to the lowliest English official or soldier, the new regime was heartily detested by the Scots. While the Anglo-Norman baronage was quiescent, the common people soon found a leader in William Wallace, younger son of a minor landowner in Ayrshire, who began his revolt at Lanark in the spring of 1297 and by midsummer had amassed a considerable army.

Wallace was a man born to be a leader. He inspired and led his men efficiently, sometimes barbarously, in a guerrilla war that was fuelled by his passion for vengeance and his love for Scotland. On 11 September he routed a much larger English army at Stirling Bridge. Afterwards, he ruled Scotland for a year in the name of the deposed King John, before he was defeated by Edward at Falkirk on 22 July 1298. Although he resigned the guardianship, Wallace continued to exert some influence on the course of affairs, and even travelled to Europe to enlist the aid of France and the Papacy.

Successive English expeditions failed to achieve any lasting result, and it was not until 1304 that Edward succeeded in retaking Stirling Castle

William Wallace ▶

which had been in Scottish hands since 1298. The Anglo-Norman baronage made their peace with Edward, and Wallace himself was captured in
1305. Taken south in chains, he was convicted of high treason and barbarously executed at Smithfield in August.

Robert Bruce, 1306–29

BORN IN ABOUT 1274, Robert Bruce was the grandson of the Competitor and son of Robert Bruce, Earl of Carrick, by his marriage to Countess Marjorie, the last of an ancient Celtic family.

THE EIGHTH GENERATION to bear the name, Robert Bruce had a typical Anglo-Norman upbringing. When Bruce submitted to Edward early in 1296, Balliol retaliated by seizing his Scottish estates and giving them to his brother-in-law, John Comyn. This was the origin of the feud between the Bruce and Balliol-Comyn factions.

In February 1306, Bruce and John 'the Red' Comyn met in Greyfriars church, Dumfries, to try to resolve their differences. A quarrel erupted and Bruce killed Comyn, compounding murder with sacrilege. Turning a desperate situation to advantage, he seized the castle of Dumfries and raised the standard of revolt. Rushing off to Scone, he had himself crowned King of Scots. In time, Bruce would go on to make Wallace's dreams of an independent

◄ *Memorial statue to Robert Bruce*

Scotland, free of English tyranny, oppression and dominance, a reality, if only for a time.

The odds were heavily stacked against him. The Balliol-Comyn faction were his deadliest enemies, he was excommunicated for the Greyfriars outrage and the clergy, hitherto the source of organised resistance to English occupation, were alienated from him. But Edward I, the Hammer of the Scots, was ailing, and his successor, the effeminate Edward II, lacked the energy or resolution to suppress the revolt.

For more than a year Bruce was on the run, but gradually his skill as a guerrilla leader developed. In March 1307 he defeated an English force at Loudoun Hill, Ayrshire. Edward I died at Burgh-on-Sands on 7 July before he could exact retribution.

▲ *Robert Bruce in battle*

Bannockburn, 1314

EDWARD II made no attempt to subjugate the Scots in the early years of his reign. Between 1307 and 1310, Robert Bruce was given a free hand to crush the Comyns and other enemies. Edward's half-hearted expedition of 1310 achieved nothing, and for a further four years Bruce, supported by Sir James 'the Black' Douglas, was allowed to consolidate his gains.

IN FEBRUARY 1310, a council of the Scottish clergy formally recognised Robert as King of Scots. By 1311 he had cleared most of the English garrisons out of Scotland and was strong enough to take the war into the enemy's territory, raiding the northern counties of England as far south as Appleby and Richmond. In 1313 he captured the castles at Roxburgh, Perth and Edinburgh. Only Stirling now remained in English hands.

In November 1313, Edward Bruce, the King's brother, laid siege to Stirling Castle. Sir Philip de Mowbray, the garrison commander, agreed to surrender if a relieving force did not arrive by 24 June 1314. At long last Edward II determined on a showdown with the Scots, but on the very day set for the surrender of the castle he sustained one of the worst defeats ever inflicted on an English army. At Bannockburn, south-east of the castle, the lightly armed Scots trounced the finest army in Europe. A score of great barons and 42 knights were slain, and 22 barons were taken prisoner. In ransom and booty alone, Bannockburn was a lucrative venture, but in terms of national prestige it proved decisive.

▲ *Battle of Bannockburn*

Declaration of Arbroath, 1320

VICTORY AT BANNOCKBURN marked the turning point in the wars of independence, although a further 14 years elapsed before the sovereignty of Scotland was acknowledged by the King of England.

IRONICALLY, IT JUSTIFIED the policy of Edward I: Scotland under a strong king was a grave menace to England under a weak king. The independence of Scotland was vindicated but Edward II foolishly refused to come to terms. The Scots took a savage revenge, raiding the northern English counties at annual intervals throughout the rest of Edward's reign.

While Robert sought in vain for a treaty with England, he strengthened his own position. At Ayr, in April 1315, he settled the succession. If he died without a son to follow him, then with the consent of his daughter Marjorie, the crown would pass to his brother Edward and his male heirs. Edward Bruce, campaigning against the English in Ulster, was crowned King of Ireland in May 1316, however he was killed in battle at Dundalk in 1318.

In 1317, Pope John XXII sent two cardinals to England to negotiate a truce between the Scots and English, but Edward II remained obdurate. In 1318, the Scots retook Berwick and in 1319 defeated an army led by the Archbishop of York at Mytton.

In response to papal overtures, an assembly of the Scottish barons, clergy and laity met at Arbroath and drew up a document addressed to the

Pope, reaffirming their independence and support for King Robert, though they asserted defiantly that they would not obey him if he ever gave way to England. The Declaration of Arbroath was the crowning achievement of Robert Bruce.

▼Arbroath Abbey

Treaty of Northampton, 1328

AFTER THE Declaration of Arbroath, the Pope annulled the king's excommunication (caused by his refusal to negotiate), but recognition of Scotland's independence was still withheld by Edward II.

BESET BY INCREASING problems at home, however, Edward was powerless to retaliate immediately, but in 1322 he led an expedition which invaded the Lothians and got as far as Edinburgh. The scorched-earth policy of the Scots denied his troops the opportunity to forage, and in the end they were driven back by hunger. In retreat, they were mercilessly harried as far as Yorkshire. A truce was arranged in May 1323, though Edward refused to recognise Bruce as King.

In 1327, Edward II was deposed by his wife and her lover and murdered shortly afterwards. The Scots under Douglas and Randolph (see p.128) raided north England and the boy-king, Edward III, campaigned in southern Scotland ineffectually. In December, Edward's regents

▲ *Edward II*

▲ *Edward III*

put out peace feelers; this led to the treaty of Northampton in May 1328.

Under its terms, the Scots won everything for which they had fought since 1307: recognition as an independent sovereign nation, ruled by a king who owed no fealty or homage to any other ruler. To seal the bargain, Edward's sister Joanna was betrothed to Bruce's five-year-old son, David. The English, however, were bitterly aware of what they were surrendering, and they would soon call it the 'Shameful Peace'. Having seen his country settled at last, King Robert retired to his palace at Cardross where he died on 7 June 1329 at the age of 56, worn out by his incessant labours and afflicted by a wasting disease. On his orders, his heart was removed from his body and placed into a silver casket.

David II, 1329–71

ON THE DEATH of Robert I, Thomas Randolph, Earl of Moray, was appointed regent for the five-year-old David II. The nephew of the late King, he proved an able administrator and an energetic soldier, but he showed a lack of statesmanship in one important respect. Going against the wishes of the dead King, he refused to restore the estates of the Comyn and Balliol families, as well as those Anglo-Norman barons who had collaborated with the English.

INEVITABLY, THE Disinherited Knights, as they came to be known, formed the nucleus of the opposition to the Bruce faction and turned to Edward III for support. Edward III was 15 when he came to power, and his mother and her lover, Mortimer (some say Edward's actual father), ruled his country for him. In 1330, Edward overthrew his mother and Mortimer, assumed the reins of government, and embarked on a renewal of the war with the Scots.

In 1331, Edward invited Edward Balliol, son and heir of the late King John, to come from Picardy to England. The following summer, Edward Balliol mustered an army in which the Disinherited Knights played a prominent part, and landed at Fife in an attempt to regain his father's throne.

Randolph raised an army to defend the realm but died at Musselburgh on 20 July 1332. Donald, Earl of Mar, was appointed regent in his place but soon proved no match for Balliol. The two armies clashed at Dupplin Moor on 12 August. Mar was killed and his forces soundly defeated. Balliol captured Perth and was crowned at Scone by the Bishop of Dunkeld.

▲ *Scone Abbey as it is today*

Halidon Hill, 1333

AT ROXBURGH, on 23 November 1332, Edward Balliol formally acknowledged Edward III as his feudal superior. The Scots, angered at this turning back of the clock, immediately rose up in revolt.

THEY CHOSE as regent Sir Andrew Moray of Bothwell, who raised another army led this time by Randolph's second son, now Earl of Moray, and Archibald Douglas, brother of Black James. Before Edward III could mount an expedition in support of his vassal, the Scots fell upon Balliol's forces near Annan, killed his younger brother and drove him back across the border in complete disarray.

The following spring, Balliol invaded Scotland and laid siege to Berwick. In the ensuing campaign, the regent and Sir William Douglas were captured by the English in separate skirmishes. Meanwhile, Edward III himself came north and joined in the siege of Berwick. In a vain attempt to relieve the town, Sir Archibald Douglas, the new regent of Scotland, attacked the English at Halidon Hill near Berwick on 19 July. In the resulting debacle, the regent, six earls and the flower of Scottish knighthood were killed. Even worse for Scotland's newly won independence was the defection of large numbers of Scottish nobles and clergy to the winning side, with the result that the Lowlands were quickly overrun by the English.

This crushing blow left Scotland worse off than it had been at any time since 1296. While David II and Queen Joanna escaped to safety in

France, Balliol relinquished Berwick for all time. At Newcastle, in June 1334, he even surrendered Scotland south of the Forth, henceforth administered as part of England.

▲ *Berwick Upon Tweed today*

David II in France, 1334–41

FOR SEVEN YEARS David and his girl-queen lived in France. For much of this period Scotland was in a state of anarchy.

EDWARD BALLIOL never established himself as an effective ruler, despite repeated expeditions by Edward III to pacify the unruly Scots. Balliol's difficulties stemmed from the Disinherited Knights who, having regained their lands, fell out among themselves, some siding with Balliol and others supporting David II. The return of Sir Andrew Moray from captivity and the Earl of Moray from France strengthened the nationalist cause. Furthermore King Philip VI of France, who gave sanctuary to the young King and Queen, made it clear that he identified with their interests.

Balliol was ousted by the patriotic faction and only restored with great difficulty by his overlord. Edward III led two other expeditions against the Scots in support of his vassal, but in 1337 he declared himself King of France, thereby starting the Hundred Years' War. Immediately he lost interest in Balliol and made no further attempt to defend the territory between the Tweed and the Forth which was nominally under his control.

In the ensuing four years, the Scots gradually won back their country. In 1338, Sir Andrew Moray died and was succeeded as regent by Robert the Steward of Scotland, son of the King's half-sister Marjorie Bruce. Perth capitulated in August 1339, and the castles of Stirling and Edinburgh soon followed. With the aid of the French, Robert cleared Scotland of invaders north of the Forth, and by 1341 it was safe enough for David and Joanna to return from their voluntary exile.

▲ *Edward III, who led two expeditions against the Scots*

The Auld Alliance

THE ALLIANCE between the Scots and France, which began in 1295 and lasted, off and on, until 1560, seldom, if ever, worked to the Scottish advantage.

IT HAD BEGUN at the time of Edward I's Gascon expedition and had induced John Balliol to defy his overlord, but on that occasion the help given by Philip IV had been minimal. Just when Scotland needed French aid the most (in 1303), Philip came to terms with Edward I. The alliance was revived in 1334 when Philip VI gave his protection to David and Joanna. This debt was more than amply repaid 12 years later.

In 1346, when the war between England and France entered a crucial phase, Edward III offered to restore those parts of Scotland still under English occupation, in exchange for a guarantee of Scottish neutrality. Despite the obvious advantages of such an arrangement, the Scots spurned Edward's offer and remained loyal to the French alliance, convinced that there could never be any lasting peace with England, and that the only guarantee of Scottish independence was a continuation of the alliance with England's natural enemy.

If the English conquered France they would soon turn against a helpless Scotland. If they were baulked in France, the English would compensate by attacking Scotland anyway. It seemed in Scotland's best interests, in the long term, to maintain the alliance, although often, in the short term, it was to prove disastrous.

▲ *Battle of Crecy, 1346*

Neville's Cross, 1346

THE AULD ALLIANCE first came into play as a factor in European power politics in the summer of 1346, when David II, in the first independent action taken as monarch, displayed that singular lack of judgment which would be the hallmark of his reign.

AFTER THE FRENCH army had been soundly defeated at Crecy, the King of France desperately needed Scottish aid to defeat England. However, instead of helping the French, David took advantage of Edward of England being occupied in France – he led his army across the border and ravaged the northern counties of England. The Archbishop of York, with Ralph Neville and Henry Percy, raised an army and fought the Scottish at Neville's Cross, near Durham, on 17 October. The Scots fought bravely but were out-manoeuvred, their phalanxes of spearmen decimated by English archers. Defeat was decisive and David was among those taken prisoner.

▲ *Battle at Neville's Cross*

For 11 years he languished in captivity. During this time Scotland was governed by the stronger Robert the Steward, though much of the country south of the Forth remained in English hands. To add to Scotland's woes, the country was ravaged by the Black Death in 1350–51 and up to a third of the population perished.

In 1354, Edward III proposed to release David on payment of a ransom. The Scots were disposed to accept these terms, but the French intervened, sent an expeditionary force to Scotland and persuaded their allies to invade England again. In 1355, the Scots and French briefly captured Berwick before Edward counter-attacked, putting every town, village and hamlet in the Lowlands to the torch.

▲ *David's defeat at the Battle of Durham*

The Release of David II

THE SACKING OF southern Scotland, known as the Burnt Candlemas, was the prelude to the negotiations that resulted in the release of David II.

BY THE TREATY of Berwick (3 October 1357), the weak David was repatriated on payment of 10,000 marks a year for 10 years. This proved an intolerable burden on a country impoverished by incessant warfare. Edward then sat back and waited for developments.

David, who had spent 11 formative years at the English court and had made many friends there, readily agreed to Edward's proposal that the ransom could be waived if he were prepared to acknowledge an English prince as his heir. When David put this proposal before a Scottish parliament in 1364 it was contemptuously rejected.

Instead, parliament sought ways and means of raising the hated ransom, and extended its deliberations beyond the barons and chief clergy to the delegates from the royal burghs, now rising in importance. Though the Third Estate had little influence on royal policy, it played an increasingly important role in forming and enacting statutes governing trade and industry, commerce, law and order.

Joanna died in 1362 and David remarried in 1364. David later divorced Margaret Logie (aunt of Annabella Drummond, who married Robert III) and she petitioned the Pope to have the divorce revoked; but David died on 22 February 1371 before papal judgment was given.

▲ *David II*

Robert II, 1371-90

DAVID died childless, and was succeeded by his nephew Robert the Steward, who became the first monarch of the Stewart line. This was the beginning of a period in which successive kings clashed with their baronage for real power and the control of national policies.

ROBERT II WAS 55 and in poor health when he came to the throne, no longer the figure he had been when in opposition, and though his reign was largely taken up in the continuing struggle with England he took no part in the actual fighting. Also, his Norman background did not possess the prestige of eight centuries of Scottish kingship. As a result, he set in motion what was to curse Scotland for centuries to come: conflict between Crown and nobility. Fortunately Edward III (who died in 1377) had little stomach for Scottish campaigns, while his successor, Richard II, was often beset by domestic problems. Nevertheless, shortly after Edward's death, the Scots made a determined effort to drive out the remaining English garrisons, and this provoked punitive expeditions by John of Gaunt and Richard himself.

In 1385, Jean de Vienne, Admiral of France, came to Scotland with a large fleet and 2,000 men as part of a Franco-Scottish expedition against England, but the campaign was inconclusive and followed by swift English retribution. In 1388, Sir William Douglas raided Ireland and the Isle of Man, and then joined an army of 40,000 which invaded Northumberland. Returning laden with booty, they were intercepted at Otterburn. Douglas

Richard II contending with the Peasants' Revolt ▶

was killed and Hotspur, son of the Earl of Northumberland, was captured. Though regarded as a Scottish victory its outcome was indecisive.

Robert III, 1390-1406

ROBERT II died in 1390 in his 74th year: 'a tenderer heart might no man have', was the verdict of a contemporary. His successor was his elder son John, Earl of Carrick, who took the regnal title of Robert III.

ALREADY 50 AND a cripple when he came to the throne, he described himself self-deprecatingly as 'the worst of kings and most wretched of men'. Feeble and passive, he was content to leave the

▲ *Dunkeld Cathedral, burial place of the Wolf of Badenoch*

government of Scotland in the hands of his advisers. His younger brother Robert, Earl of Fife, had been appointed regent in 1388 and Robert III was happy to leave this arrangement in place. Despite his savage self-assessment, however, Robert III was personally popular and in the early years the country enjoyed a peace it had not experienced since the reign of Alexander III.

The alliance with France was renewed in 1390, while an eight-year truce with England meant that, apart from the usual cross-border raids, serious warfare was avoided. In the Highlands, however, there were outbreaks of disorder in which the King's brother Alexander, Earl of Buchan – better known to posterity as the Wolf of Badenoch – played a sinister part. In 1396, teams of 30 men from the powerful clans Chattan and Kay settled a long-running feud in a pitched battle on the North Inch at Perth before a large crowd of spectators: the 30 men on each side were entering themselves as champions for their resepctive clans, deciding their differences by sword and no other weapon. The defeated clan was to be pardoned for all its former offences, and the winners honoured with royal favour. This bloody encounter ended with the death of all but 12 of the combatants.

North Inch, Perth today ▼

Albany, Rothesay and the Regency

FROM 1399 onwards, the reign of Robert III was dominated by the struggle for the regency, between the King's brother and his elder son.

▲ *Rothesay Window, Falkland Palace*

I N 1398, THE KING'S eldest son David, Earl of Carrick, was created Duke of Rothesay. At the same time, his uncle, Robert of Fife, received the title of Duke of Albany, the ancient name for northern Scotland. In January 1399, Rothesay was put in charge of the country north of the Forth and Clyde, and soon afterwards, with the help of his scheming mother and Archibald the Grim, third Earl of Douglas, he ousted his uncle and became regent.

In the same year, Richard II was deposed and succeeded in England by Henry IV. When the Scots rejected a renewal of the truce and began raiding across the border, Henry led an army against them, the last English monarch to do so in person. The campaign was inconsequential, though the inability of the Scottish generals, Albany and Rothesay, to act in concert might have made matters worse.

This triggered off a bitter feud in which the magnates and lesser barons took sides. In 1401, Rothesay, unpopular and dissolute, was deposed and Albany regained power. The following year Rothesay escaped but was recaptured and died in mysterious circumstances at Falkland (some sources claim that he was killed by his uncle).

The border war escalated in 1402. The Scots, under Murdoch Stewart, son of Albany, and Archibald, the young Earl of Douglas, penetrated as far as Newcastle but were routed at Homildon Hill.

▲ *Doune Castle, built by Robert, Duke of Albany*

Robert, Duke of Albany, 1406–20

IN 1406, fearing for his 12-year-old younger son James, the King sent him to France for safety, but the boy was captured at sea by the English and remained a prisoner for 18 years. Robert III died on receiving this news, and once more Scotland was plunged into a long regency for a king in captivity.

JAMES I WAS A PRISONER until 1424. For most of that time Robert, Duke of Albany was regent. Although 70 when he assumed the regency in 1406, he ruled with a firm hand. Unlike previous regents, Albany ruled in his own name, but the chroniclers are unanimous in stating that he governed Scotland wisely and well. He showed consid-

erable tact and statesmanship in his handling of the nobility, securing the release from English captivity of the Earl of Douglas and persuading the Earl of March (who had aided and abetted Henry IV) to return from exile.

Although hampered by the fact that his own son Murdoch, as well as James I, was being held hostage by the English, Albany managed to retake both Jedburgh (1409) and Fast Castle (1410). In 1415, the Scots burned Penrith and, as a result, the English destroyed Dumfries in revenge. In 1416, a two-pronged attack by Albany and Douglas on Berwick and Roxburgh achieved little. Murdoch was freed that year, in exchange for the Earl of Northumberland.

Albany died in 1420, having, in effect, ruled Scotland for almost half a century. Posterity has judged that, on the whole, he administered Scotland efficiently. He was succeeded as regent by his son Murdoch, who failed to control the unruly magnates. It was not long before the country fell rapidly into a state of disorder.

Berwick Upon Tweed, attacked by Albany and Douglas ▼

St Andrews University

IN 1406, the Lollard preacher James Resby, a follower of John Wycliffe, was burned at Perth as a heretic, the earliest evidence of the reform movement in Scotland. To counter the spread of such heresy, Scotland's first university was founded by Bishop Wardlaw at St Andrews in 1411.

HITHERTO, SCOTTISH students had gone abroad for their higher education. In times of peace they went south, to Oxford and Cambridge, but as a reflection of the Auld Alliance increasingly they went to France from the early fourteenth century onwards. In 1326, the Bishop of Moray founded the Scots College in Paris.

Lectures in canon law and theology were being delivered at St Andrews by 1410 and though the papal document formally establishing the university was not delivered till February 1414 it is now generally accepted that the university had its foundation in 1411.

This year was also memorable for the battle fought at Harlaw, Aberdeenshire, sometimes regarded as a decisive struggle between Celt and Saxon. In fact it was fought between

Donald of the Isles, a grandson of Robert II who claimed the earldom of Ross in right of his wife. Having defeated the Frasers and Mackays who opposed his claim, Donald advanced on Aberdeen, whose citizens marched out to do battle under the command of Alexander Stewart, son of the Wolf of Badenoch and now Earl of Mar. Defeated in one of Scotland's bloodiest battles, Donald was pursued by Albany and for a time the Highlands were pacified.

▲ *St Salvator's Quad, St Andrews University*

A Parliamentary System Established

UNLIKE ENGLAND, where a parliamentary system involving the nobility, clergy and burgesses was established at Westminster in 1295, Scotland only gradually evolved an assembly which represented the people as a whole.

AS FAR BACK AS 1326, Robert Bruce convened a parliament at Cambuskenneth at which, for the first time, the magnates and prelates were joined by delegates from the burghs, but representation of all Three Estates was not given formal recognition till a century later. In 1428, James I, who had returned from his long detention in England four years earlier, took an important step towards giving Scotland more truly representative government.

In order to gain backing for a package of administrative reforms, he expanded his Council by a statute which laid down that two 'wise men' from each county should be chosen by the lesser landowners to represent them and that they should elect 'a Common Speaker of the Parliament'. This parliament,

◀ *Robert Bruce*

▲ *Cambuskenneth Abbey*

which met at Perth, was the most important of the 13 convened by James during the rest of his reign. Altogether, these parliaments enacted a lengthy series of measures for the better administration of the kingdom.

These Acts ranged from compulsory archery practice for the defence of the realm to the establishment of inns, the cultivation of peas and beans, the destruction of wolves, the care of lepers and the sale of salmon. It was a long time, however, before the government was strong enough to enforce them.

James II, 1437-60

AT PERTH in February 1437, James I fell victim to a conspiracy led by Sir Robert Graham. Eight assassins burst into the King's chamber as he was undressing for bed and stabbed him to death. Retribution was swift, and the torture and death of the murderers was lingering and barbaric even by the standards of the time.

HIS SUCCESSOR, JAMES II, was six years old; during his long minority Scotland was subjected to virtual civil war between the Douglas and Stewart factions and the struggles of Sir Alexander Livingstone and Sir William Crichton for control of the boy-king. In this turbulent period much of the progress in central government was undone.

In 1449, James II came of age and married Mary of Gueldres, reinforcing the French connection. James had a bloody showdown with the Douglases, personally stabbing the eighth Earl to

▲ *Catherine Douglas tries to protect James I, 1437*

death at Stirling Castle in February 1452. Parliament dutifully recorded that the Earl was guilty of his own death 'by resisting the King's gentle persuasions'. In 1453 and 1455, James campaigned vigorously against the Douglas faction, pillaging their lands ruthlessly.

Taking advantage of an England weakened by troubles of their own with the long and bitter rivalry for the throne, the Wars of the Roses, James also recovered the rest of southern Scotland, expelling the English garrison from Roxburgh in 1460. It was a fateful move for him to have made however, for while besieging the castle, the 29-year-old James was killed when one of his newfangled cannon exploded.

Stirling Castle ▼

James III, 1460–88

JAMES III was only nine years old, so once again Scotland faced the uncertainties of a long minority, but fortunately the country was ruled wisely by Bishop Kennedy of St Andrews. The Scots even succeeded in obtaining the return of Berwick, ceded in 1464 by Henry VI in return for help to the Lancastrian cause.

JAMES ASSUMED POWER in 1469 in propitious circumstances. Scotland was at peace with England, and the power of the great magnates had been crushed. The marriage of James to Anne of Denmark brought Orkney and Shetland as her dowry. St Andrews was raised to an archbishopric in 1472; and in 1476 the rebellious Lord of the Isles was finally brought to heel.

James III, however, was uninterested in the affairs of state, and so hardly the person to restore the confidence and strength the monarchy needed. To protect his throne from plotters, he imprisoned both his brothers, Albany and

◀ *Henry VI of England*

Mar. Peace and progress were marred by the factiousness of the nobles who sided with the Duke of Albany. Albany escaped and fled to France, intrigued with the Earl of Douglas (in exile in England), and formed an alliance with Edward IV, promising to be his vassal if Edward secured him the Scottish throne.

In 1482, Albany, now styled Alexander IV, invaded southern Scotland with an English army led by the Duke of Gloucester (the future Richard III) who captured Berwick, thereafter in English hands for ever. James's forces mutinied at Lauder, and under the leadership of the Earl of Angus (head of the Red Douglas faction) hanged the King's favourites and came to terms with Albany.

▲ *Berwick Upon Tweed: returned by Henry VI; retaken by the Duke of Gloucester*

Sauchieburn, 1488

JAMES was escorted back to Edinburgh and detained in the castle, but by a treaty of August 1482 Albany undertook to give his allegiance to his brother on condition of being restored to his titles and estates.

EFFECTIVELY, HOWEVER, the government was now in the hands of Albany, the Archbishop of St Andrews, the Bishop of Dunkeld and a handful of magnates, while the King remained in detention. Albany and his confederates soon quarrelled. Albany freed his brother and for a time harmony was restored, but Alexander fled into exile again. In 1484, he returned with an English army but was defeated at Lochmaben and fled to France, where he was killed in a tournament a year later. His ally, the ninth Earl of Douglas was taken prisoner and died at Lindores.

Four years later, James's misgovernment, his preference for English favourites as advisers and the resentment of the nobility who had suffered forfeiture for aiding Albany, led to a rebellion involving the Earls of Angus and Argyll and many of the leading barons. The King's heir, the Duke of Rothesay, was seized by the rebels and brought to the field of battle against his father at Sauchieburn near Stirling on 11 June 1488. James had not wanted to fight, but was forced to do so when the city of Stirling refused to give him refuge. He was defeated and escaped, but was discovered in hiding and murdered in cold blood, stabbed by a passer-by claiming to be a priest.

The rebellion of 1488 was significant in that it was directed against the King as a person, and not the dynasty. The rebels justified their actions by invoking the name of the King's son.

▲ *Falkland Palace, home of the Rothesay family*

James IV, 1488-1513

THE REBELS justified their actions on political grounds, and followed with an assertion of parliamentary authority aiming at constitutional government. This tendency did not survive the assumption of power by James IV, a boy of fifteen at the time of his father's death.

THE NEW KING'S ADVISERS went to great pains to justify their actions, in a document circulated to the papacy and the leading powers of Europe. At home, revolts in the name of the murdered King were swiftly put down. By 1490 James had assumed control of the government and proved to be an able and energetic ruler. He governed wisely but firmly, swift to act against any hint of rebellion. In May 1493 he annexed to the crown the title of Lord of the Isles and personally established royal authority in the Hebrides by a grand tour of the islands the following August.

Having restored peace at home, James had ambitions to take his rightful place among the great European rulers. To the old alliance with France were added his personal connections: his mother was Danish and his paternal grandmother Burgundian. He was a prince of the Renaissance, taking a great interest in art, music and architecture, but he also built a navy which, under Andrew Wood, achieved considerable success against English pirates – it was the start of a Scottish shipbuilding industry that was to become the envy of the world in years to come. Allied to the Emperor Maximilian and the Duchess of Burgundy, James sup-

Emperor Maximilian I of Germany ▶

ported the claims of Perkin Warbeck to the English throne, and in 1496 and 1497 he half-hearted-ly invaded England in support of the pretender.

The Union of the Thistle and the Rose, 1503

IN HIS BID to isolate France by a series of diplomatic marriages, Ferdinand of Aragon promised James a Spanish princess. When this never materialised, similar negotiations with England, long drawn out and dilatory between July 1499 and January 1502, led eventually to the marriage of James and Margaret Tudor, daughter of Henry VII, on 8 August 1503.

THE BRIDE WAS not quite 15 at the time of the marriage, romantically dubbed the Union of the Thistle and the Rose. The ceremony took place at Holyrood Palace, Edinburgh, and was attended by many dignitaries from England. Out of this union would come, a century later, the union of the crowns and then, more than a century further on, the union of the parliaments. The treaty of 1502 which arranged the marriage was, in fact, the first real peace between Scotland

Heraldic panel, Holyrood Palace ▶

and England since the Treaty of Northampton, broken in 1332.

The marriage brought no advantage and little personal happiness to James who made it clear to his father-in-law that he would not be ruled by him. Relations with England deteriorated after Henry VII died in 1509, and James was on increasingly bad terms with his brother-in-law, Henry VIII, whose refusal to hand over part of Margaret's dowry was one of the vexatious matters that would lead to Flodden.

Nevertheless, for 15 years (1496–1512) the two countries were at peace and in that period Scotland enjoyed considerable commercial growth. The only serious disturbance came from Donald Dhu of the Isles whose revolt in the Highlands and Islands lasted four years (1503–06).

▲ *Henry VII of England*

Flodden, 1513

FERDINAND'S Holy League against France caused grave disquiet to James who suddenly realised that if France were destroyed, Scotland would be at the mercy of the victors.

HIS FEARS WERE more imaginary than real. Although Henry VIII had allied himself to Spain by marrying Katherine of Aragon, he balanced this by marrying his younger sister to Louis XII of France. By 1512, Scotland and England were virtually at war on the high seas, and Henry's expedition to Guienne in June finally convinced James to throw in his lot with France.

▲ *Flodden Field today*

Against the advice of his counsellors, he embarked on a collision course with Henry. Far from acting as a mediator, Queen Margaret backed her husband, angered at her brother's refusal to hand over jewels which rightfully belonged to her. Finally, a resumption of border raids determined James on a showdown. Mustering the largest army Scotland had ever seen, he led it into battle on a remote Cheviot hillside. At Flodden, the Scots fought ferociously and desperately but their opponents had the tactical advantage. Scottish bravery proved no match against the English, who used artillery and the new long English bills to great advantage against the shorter spears and swords of the Scots. King James and the flower of Scottish chivalry were slaughtered: 13 earls, 14 lords, an archbishop, a bishop, two abbots and numerous knights perished that day, and there was hardly a noble family that had not suffered loss. The gallantry of James's death mitigated the folly which caused it.

James V, 1513-42

THE NATIONAL spirit may have been uplifted by its heroism, but there is no escaping the fact that Flodden was a major disaster. James's heir was a baby, the best of the country's leaders had been killed, and once more Scotland endured the misery of a long minority. The much-vaunted navy was sold to the French and Scotland did not recover its prosperity for over a century.

UNTIL 1528, SCOTLAND was governed by a succession of regents. A measure of the desperate situation was the appointment of Alexander of Albany, the son of the traitor Duke. Born and bred in France, Albany spoke nothing but French and actually spent most of his regency (1515–24) in Paris. Queen Margaret married the Earl of Angus who intrigued with the Earl of Arran to govern Scotland till 1528, when the young King escaped his stepfather's clutches and assumed the reins of power.

James's effective reign was dominated by closer alignment with France and the corresponding enmity of Henry VIII. James was married twice, to Madeleine, daughter of Francis I of France, and then to Mary of Guise. He attempted to limit the absolute power of the nobles by introducing reforms. Naturally, this was not well received, and to make matters more difficult for him, he was distracted by England. Henry persisted in trying to alienate James from the French connection, and undermine the influence of Cardinal Beaton, leader of the Catholic faction, after Henry broke with the papacy. When the Scots invaded

Henry VIII of England ▶

England in November 1542, they were routed at Solway Moss. Poor health had prevented James from participating, and news of the disaster hastened his death on 14 December.

Mary, Queen of Scots

IN 1542, ON HEARING that his wife had given birth to a daughter a week earlier, James V is said to have commented, 'it came with a lass, and it'll gang with a lass', a reference to Marjorie Bruce whose son founded the Stewart dynasty.

N OT SATISFIED WITH JUST Wales added to his kingdom, Henry VIII wanted Scotland too. The death of his nephew provided him with a chance for closer ties to Scotland, but by his arrogance and impatience he mismanaged matters. The proposal that the infant Mary, Queen of Scots, should marry Henry's son and heir, Edward, the young, sickly prince (who died in 1553), was not unwelcome; but Henry followed it with unreasonable demands which the Scots angrily rejected. Henry then retaliated by ordering the Earl of Hertford (later Duke of Somerset) to ravage the Lowlands and Border counties in a series of campaigns which the Scots wrily called the

John Knox Window, St Giles' Cathedral ▶

'Rough Wooing'. Somerset's victory at Pinkie Cleugh in September 1547 failed in its objective of severing the Auld Alliance.

Meanwhile, the reformers (see p.172), led by John Knox, murdered Cardinal Beaton at St Andrews in 1546, and held the castle with English aid against the forces of the Queen Mother. In this way the political and religious factors polarised, with the Protestant, pro-English faction ranged against the Catholic, pro-French faction of Mary of Guise. When the castle of St Andrews surrendered in July 1547 the reformers were executed or sent to the French galleys.

Mary in France, 1548–61

INITIALLY, the infant-queen, Mary, was to be promised to Edward VI in marriage. This struck fear into Scottish hearts, believing it would lead to England's annexing of Scotland. To avoid this, the Earl of Arran opened negotiations for a marriage treaty, whereby Mary would marry the Dauphin Francis. For her safety, the little Queen of Scots was sent to France in August 1548, where she remained for 13 years.

FOR MOST OF THAT time Mary was under the care and protection of her mother's relations, the powerful Guise family, but was brought up with the princes and princesses of the reigning Valois dynasty. Destined for matrimony from early childhood, Mary and the Dauphin had a genuine affection for each other. Their marriage in Notre Dame in April 1558 was a glittering occasion.

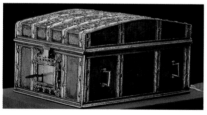

The death of Henry II of France in 1559 as a result of a jousting accident brought the Dauphin to the throne as Francis II, and briefly Mary was Queen of both Scotland and France. Unwisely, Mary had also assumed the lions of England in her arms, following the death of the Catholic Mary Tudor in 1558 and the accession of Elizabeth, who was denounced as a heretic and a bastard.

▲ *Silver casket belonging to Mary*

In December 1560, Francis II died, leaving his widow and her Guise uncles at the mercy of the Queen Mother, Catherine de Medicis. Her position in France increasingly untenable, Mary decided to go back to the land of her birth. In August 1561, Mary returned to Scotland. In political and religious terms, however, it had changed radically since she had last seen it.

▼ *'Bloody Mary'*

The Regency of the Queen Mother

AFTER MARY, QUEEN OF SCOTS sailed to France, her mother remained in Scotland. French troops helped the Scots to evict English garrisons, and the Auld Alliance seemed stronger than ever.

THE EARL OF ARRAN was induced to hand over the regency to the Queen Mother; in return for this action he was given the French title of Duke of Chatelherault. Mary of Guise surrounded herself with French advisers and troops, and Scotland soon found itself being treated as a French dependency, like Brittany or Navarre. The Scots would have been even more alarmed had they known that their girl-queen had been persuaded to sign away her throne as part of her marriage agreement in 1558. Should she die without producing a son, the succession to the Scottish throne would automatically pass to the King of France and his heirs, in flagrant contravention of assurances by Henry II to the Scottish parliament.

Anti-French feeling was stirred up by the religious reformers, aided and abetted by England. In 1557, the Protestant faction formed the Congregation of the Lord and signed the first National Covenant. In 1559, they solemnly deposed the Queen Regent and formally asked Queen Elizabeth to take the realm of Scotland under her protection.

Mary of Guise, worn out and terminally ill, died at Edinburgh Castle in June 1560, while an English fleet was besieging Leith. Her death effectively brought the Auld Alliance to an end.

Relics of Mary, Queen of Scots ▶

Scottish History

 The Reformation

ELIZABETH OF ENGLAND never forgave her cousin's insult of assuming the English arms. She also realised that it was in her interests to support the Scottish reformers against the authority of Mary of Guise.

THE LOWLANDS OF SCOTLAND were ripe for the spread of Protestantism, for it was where most of Scotland's wealth and power was concentrated, where the influence of the English was felt most strongly. Unfortunately for the Queen Mother, she chose that moment to come down hard on the Protestant faction who were denounced as heretics. The Lords of the Congregation retaliated by the wholesale destruction of monasteries and churches in Perth. Although she promised not to send French troops to that town, she went in person with her bodyguard, and this was regarded as a highly provocative act. The destruction of religious houses escalated in the ensuing months.

The death of the Queen Mother in June 1560 placed the Lords of the Congregation in the ascendant. A parliament, of dubious legality, was called and rushed through a series of measures, abolishing Roman Catholicism and prohibiting the practice of that religion on pain of death. Doubtless many of the powerful figures who formed the Lords of the Congregation had no doctrinal interest in the new faith, but were influenced by the prospect of seizing ecclesiastical lands; but there is no doubting the fanaticism of the movement's spiritual leader, John Knox, who aimed at establishing a theocracy along the lines of the Calvinists in

Protestant reformer, John Knox ▶

Geneva. With William Maitland of Lethington and Lord James Stewart (Mary's illegitimate half-brother), Knox formed the triumvirate that ruled Scotland after the Queen Mother's death.

Mary's Personal Rule, 1561–67

WHEN MARY and her entourage landed at Leith in August 1561 there was no one there to meet them. It was an ill omen for her personal reign which lasted less than six years.

JUST 18 AND A WIDOW, she was no longer Queen of France but throroughly French in outlook and education. Mary began in a spirit of conciliation. Accepting the situation, she relied heavily on the advice of her half-brother, whom she made Earl of Moray. She was hard-headed enough to realise that there could be no Counter-Reformation, though she hoped that some spirit of toleration would permit Catholics to practise their faith unmolested. But even her celebration of Mass in the privacy of her own chapel caused a furore, and Mary, in a series of confrontations with Knox, found him obdurate.

The Catholic cause was undermined by the treasonable behaviour of the Earl of Huntly, the leading Catholic magnate. Mary herself took part in the campaign of 1562 which led to Huntly's downfall.

A widow barely out of her teens, Mary was the subject of intense matrimonial speculation. Several foreign princes were put forward (or suggested themselves) as suitable suitors. Marriage to Don Carlos of Spain, the Archduke of Austria, or her young brother-in-law, Charles of France, would have strengthened Mary in Scotland, but undermined her position as heiress presumptive to the English throne. Nine years younger than Elizabeth, Mary strenuously sought recognition of her claim, should Elizabeth die without issue. This matter would dominate relations between the cousins for many years.

Mary, Queen of Scots' house, Jedburgh ▶

The Murders of Riccio and Darnley

ELIZABETH suggested that Mary should marry an English noble-man, and even proposed her own lover, Robert Dudley, for this role. For several years she amused herself with insincere sugges-tions of this sort.

WHEN MARY TOOK the initiative and, in 1565, chose as her husband – seemingly with a complete lack of foresight – her cousin Henry Stewart, Lord Darnley. Elizabeth was furious. Mary and Darnley were the grandchildren of Margaret Tudor. Darnley's father Matthew, Earl of Lennox, was a son of Margaret's second marriage, to the Earl of Angus. He was there-fore next after Mary herself in the line of succession to the English throne. Elizabeth retaliated by aiding Moray in an abortive rebellion.

With his lust for power, Darnley (styled King Henry) soon proved a bad choice of husband. Foolish, vain, debauched and dissolute, he was manipulated by certain lords who plotted the murder of Mary's Italian secretary, David Riccio. Formerly valet to the

Elizabeth I of England ▶

Savoyard ambassador, Riccio became the Queen's favourite, though rumours of sexual impropriety are unfounded. Riccio's murder on 9 March 1566 was followed shortly by a plot to murder Darnley himself, while he was convalescing from a serious illness, on Mary's advice, at Kirk O'Field. On the night of 10 February 1567, the house was destroyed by an explosion, but Darnley and his servant were later found strangled in a nearby orchard. Suspicion for the murder fell on James Hepburn, Earl of Bothwell, whom Mary married. The question of Mary's complicity in the crime has been fiercely debated to this day.

▲ *Mary's part in the murder of Darnley remains a mystery.*

Bothwell

JAMES HEPBURN, fourth Earl of Bothwell, Lord High Admiral of Scotland, emerged as the strong man of Scotland after the Darnley murder. Though accused of the murder by Darnley's father, the Earl of Lennox, Bothwell was declared to be not guilty by a court packed with his supporters and for a time his faction was in the ascendant.

RUMOURS (and mysterious placards posted on the buildings of Edinburgh in the dead of night) suggested that the Queen was involved in her husband's death. On her return from Stirling, where she had visited her baby son, Mary was abducted by Bothwell, allegedly raped by him, and left with no alternative but to marry him, on 15 May 1567. Bothwell, about 10 years her senior, was not without a certain roguish charm. Recently married to Lady Jean Gordon (sister of the Earl of Huntly), he divorced her in order to marry Mary according to the new Protestant rites.

This moral lapse scandalised the nation and alienated many of the Protestant lords, previously Bothwell's

▲ *Mary, Queen of Scots*

conspirators, as well as Mary's Catholic subjects. Opposition to Mary and
Bothwell gathered momentum and they managed to alienate many previous supporters. Eventually the couple withdrew to Bothwell's stronghold
at Dunbar. On 15 June, the Marian and rebel armies met at Carberry Hill;
deserted by many of her supporters, Mary had no alternative but to surrender, though Bothwell managed to escape. For a time he engaged in
piracy off the north of Scotland but was captured by the Danes and ended
his days in 1576, incarcerated in such vile conditions that he was eventually driven insane.

▲ *Edinburgh, where Mary was taken after her arrest*

Lochleven and Langside

MARY was taken, dishevelled and in her red petticoat, under guard to Edinburgh where she was reviled and humiliated by the mob. Later she was transported to Lochleven, where she was guarded by the family of Lady Margaret Douglas, mother of the Queen's half-brother Moray.

HE RETURNED FROM France on 11 August and was proclaimed regent 11 days later. From the outset his government was hampered by the opposition of important nobles like Argyll (who objected to the way Mary had been treated) and the Hamilton faction, angered that their chief had been passed over for the regency. Mary was forced to abdicate the throne to her baby son, who was crowned at Stirling on 29 July, John Knox preaching the coronation sermon.

▲ *Lochleven Castle*

On 2 May 1568, Mary escaped from her island prison, and with the aid of the Hamilton faction mustered a large army in opposition to Moray. The opposing forces clashed at Langside near Glasgow. Both sides were numerically even, but Moray's troops were better armed and led. From a nearby hill Mary watched the battle, which was short but decisive. As her supporters fled in disarray, Mary herself rode south through Dumfriesshire and Galloway to Dundrennan. Ignoring the sound advice of her remaining entourage to take ship back to the safety of France, she crossed the Solway on 16 May and landed at Workington in Cumberland.

▲ *Mary, after clashes at Langside*

Mary in England, 1568–87

AS A FUGITIVE, Mary arrived unannounced in a country which, not so long ago, she had claimed as her own. It is hardly surprising that her cousin Elizabeth should be uncertain how to treat her; was she to be an honoured guest or regarded as a dangerous subversive, a person around whom Catholic dissidents might rally to threaten Elizabeth's throne.

ELIZABETH decided to play safe, and instead of inviting Mary to her court, had her detained for 19 years in various great houses or castles in the Midlands, in conditions of increasing severity as time passed. Many attempts to liberate Mary were made by her countrymen, but to no avail. An inquiry into the Scottish rebellion was turned into a trial of Mary herself, at which she was not permitted to be present. It was at this trial between Mary and her brother that the so-called Casket Letters first made their appearance. Though now deemed to be forgeries, they swayed judgment against Mary at the time.

One of the greatest disappointments for Mary was her inability to communicate with her son as he grew to manhood. Brought up as a strict

Protestant and taught to hate and despise his mother as an adulterer and the murderer of his father, James did nothing to help her. Mary's complicity in the Babington Plot (actually engineered by Elizabeth's ministers and their agents) sealed her fate, and following a show trial at Fotheringhay Castle (where Mary handled her own defence, so it is said, with the eloquence and dignity due to a queen) she was executed in February 1587.

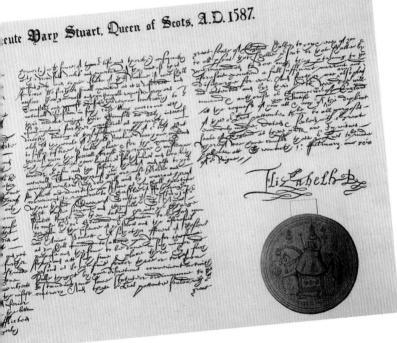

▲ *Warrant to execute Mary, Queen of Scots*

James VI and I

REGENCIES during the minority reign of James VI (1567–84).

ALTHOUGH MARY languished in capitivity in England, she was not without strong support in Scotland. Ironically, the leaders of the Marian faction were Maitland of Lethington and Sir William Kirkcaldy of Grange, the general who had defeated her at Langside. Both were staunch Protestants, and Maitland also cherished the ambition to see Scotland and England united under the same crown.

The Marian opposition gave considerable trouble to successive regents during the long minority of James VI. Moray restored law and order, suppressed abortive uprisings and dealt firmly with would-be conspirators, but in the end he was assassinated at Linlithgow on 22 January 1570, by James Hamilton of Bothwellhaugh.

He was followed by the Earl of Lennox, father of Darnley and the boy-king's grandfather, who ruled with the support of English arms. Scotland descended into civil war, in which Maitland and Kirkcaldy held Edinburgh Castle and bombarded the city. The death of Lennox during a coup and counter-coup at Stirling, on 3 September 1571, brought the Earl of Mar briefly to power. He died in October 1572 and was succeeded as regent by the Earl of Morton. Forced out of office in 1578, he briefly returned to power, but in June 1581 was executed for his part in Darnley's murder. Ruthless and unscrupulous, he nevertheless ruled Scotland well and maintained the English alliance.

▼ *During the civil war, Edinburgh Castle was held by Maitland and Kirkcaldy.*

The Ruthven Raid, 1582

WITH THE DEATH of Morton, James VI, now aged 15, took over the government himself. He relied heavily on Esme Stuart, a Catholic cousin of his late father, whom he made Duke of Lennox.

L ENNOX WAS STUBBORNLY and foolishly determined to make a Catholic of the young King, and to lead a Catholic rising in Britain with the help of France and Spain. James's choice, therefore, roused hostility, and to defuse the situation Lennox converted to Protestantism while James launched a new National Covenant that was ferociously anti-Catholic. These moves did not allay the suspicions of the Protestant extremists, further alarmed by the King's preference for episcopacy by which he sought, through bishops of his choosing, to control the Church.

On 22 August 1582, James was detained after a hunting trip and taken to the Castle of Ruthven by the Earls of Mar and Gowrie and other lords, forewarned by an English agent that Lennox meant to arrest them for Riccio's murder. As a result of the Ruthven Raid, Scotland was ruled by the conspirators for 10 months and Lennox forced to flee.

James escaped on 27 June 1583, and soon came under the spell of a new favourite, the Earl of Arran. A full pardon was offered to the Ruthven conspirators, but when they planned a revolt in April 1584 James nipped it in the bud. Gowrie, who was involved in the new conspiracy, was its chief victim, convicted as much for his part in the Ruthven Raid as in the later plot. On 2 May he was beheaded at Stirling. The other plotters fled to England, leaving Arran stronger, and more deeply detested, than Lennox had been.

▲ *Stirling Castle, where Gowrie was beheaded*

James and Elizabeth

DURING THE ASCENDANCY of Lennox, James had made tentative overtures to his mother, and had intrigued with the Guise family. He even wrote to the Pope promising his allegiance in return for support against his enemies.

AWARE THAT THE KING was flirting with Rome, the Ruthven plotters had been goaded into action. The failure of their conspiracy induced Queen Elizabeth to intrigue against James, just as she had fomented opposition to his mother and grandmother. The rise of the Catholic League in France (March 1585), however, made James apprehensive, and his success in suppressing the Ruthven plot encouraged him to reopen negotiations with Elizabeth. Arran, who had urged this course of action, was a victim of his own advice. Elizabeth distrusted him, and as part of the defensive and offensive treaty he was dismissed in November.

The treaty was ratified at Berwick in July 1586. James's adherence to the new alliance was sorely tried by the events of that year which culminated in his mother's trial and execution. Cynically observing that the dead don't bite, James did not protest at his mother's death, although popular opinion in Scotland was anti-English for a time. James calmed his indignant countrymen and took energetic steps against the Armada in 1588. Although Elizabeth never recognised him as her heir, and even intrigued with his opponents, she and James were on cordial terms in the last year of her life.

James VI ▶

James and Spain

ALTHOUGH JAMES took care not to jeopardise his claims to the English succession for the sake of his mother's life, his patience with Elizabeth understandably wore thin at times.

ELIZABETH, NINE YEARS older than Mary and unmarried, would not live for ever, and James had the strongest claim to succeed her. But Elizabeth lived to 70, a ripe old age for the period, and James, despairing of attaining the English throne and exasperated by Elizabeth's intrigues against him, retaliated with intrigues of his own.

English suspicions that James was less firmly wedded to the Protestant cause than he professed were roused by his indulgence towards the Catholic Earls of Errol and Huntly, detected by Elizabeth's intelligence service as being in contact with Spain, not long after the Armada. Three years later (1592), Elizabeth's agents procured the Spanish Blanks – blank documents bearing the signatures of Errol, Huntly and Angus. Papers accompanying these forms indicated that the Earls were drafting a treaty with Spain for a Scottish invasion of England.

James himself was privy to this plan, as borne out by a memo in his hand setting out the pros and cons of the project. Such deviousness might have disqualified James from the English throne, but for the fact that he was regarded by Sir Robert Cecil (Elizabeth's chief minister) as the least of the evils England would have to choose among on Elizabeth's death.

▲ *James feasting with Spanish ambassadors*

Religious Unrest, 1584-96

ALTHOUGH THE PROTESTANT religion was legally established by the Scottish parliament in 1567, it was many years before its position and character were secured.

JOHN KNOX, architect of the religious revolution, died in October 1572. In that year the Convention of Leith established a form of episcopacy which was regarded unfavourably by the majority of the ministers, fearing (rightly as it turned out) that this would subordinate the Church to the State.

Under Knox's successor, Andrew Melville, who returned to Scotland in 1574, the gauntlet was flung down. Melville was even more radical than Knox had been, insisting that the Church direct the affairs of state, putting divine authority before civil jurisdiction. Calling a General Assembly of ministers in August 1575, Melville challenged the doctrine of episcopacy. As a result, the bishops became administrators without powers superior to the ordinary ministers. Instead, ministers were organised in democratic bodies called presbyteries (1580).

The growth of Presbyterianism had been a constant source of friction for Morton (who died in 1581) and, later, King James, who used the Ruthven Raid as a pretext for the Black Acts of 1584, asserting his sovereignty over the Church. When the Spanish intrigues of the Catholic Earls were exposed in 1592, James was compelled to repeal the 1584 legislation by means of the Golden Act which recognised church courts. When the ministers overstepped the mark in 1596, however, James succeeded in gaining control of the General Assembly, restoring titular bishops and giving them seats in parliament.

▲ *John Knox House*

Further Plots and Conspiracies, 1587-1600

THE EXECUTION of Gowrie in May 1584 did not bring the struggle between King James and the malcontents, both religious and political, to a close. To the end of the century there would be continual plotting and intrigue, but significantly there was little real threat to the throne.

JAMES ATTEMPTED to put an end to internecine feuds by summoning the nobility to a love-feast in May 1587, then ordering the destruction of the gibbets and the release of all political prisoners. This statesmanlike approach worked for a time; but between 1591 and 1594 the peace was disturbed on several occasions by the activities of Francis, Earl of Bothwell (a nephew of Queen Mary's third husband). His swashbuckling antics culminated in a serious revolt of Catholic dissidents in the north-east, crushed by James's own resolute action in October 1594. Clan feuds in the Highlands and Islands continued for several years, though the last such battle in the Borders, between the Johnstones and Maxwells at Dryfe Sands, Dumfriesshire, took place in December 1593. The death of Lord Maxwell and the fall of the northern Earls destroyed the Catholic cause.

The Gowrie Conspiracy in August 1600 was allegedly a plot by the sons of the first Earl to kidnap the King. Both the second Earl and his brother were killed in the fray and posterity takes the view that James engineered the plot, to wreak vengeance on a troublesome family whose grandfather, Lord Ruthven, had led the murder of Riccio.

The Gowrie Conspiracy ▶

Union of the Crowns, 1603

ON THE NIGHT of 24 March 1603, Sir Robert Carey, having ridden from London in three days, brought James the news that Elizabeth was dead. Two days later word reached him that the Privy Council had declared him to be her successor.

JAMES LEFT Edinburgh on 5 April and headed south, to claim the throne he had longed for all his life, with the promise that he would return to Scotland every three years. In fact he came back only once, in 1617, and then only to meddle in Church affairs. No longer would rebel lords or religious dissidents intrigue with England or seek refuge there; as a result, much of the factiousness and conspiracy of previous generations disappeared. Instead the earls and barons resolved their quarrels and concentrated on the secularisation of Church lands to their own benefit.

Scotland was now adminstered through the King's Privy Council but all real power remained in James's hands. He greatly favoured a union of the two kingdoms, and the national flag, the Union Jack, bore the crosses of St Andrew and St George. The Highlands were pacified and the MacGregor clan outlawed for massacring their Lennox neighbours. Blood feuds were settled by heavy fines or imprisonment. Attempts to colonise Lewis (1599–1607) by 'gentlemen venturers' were a failure, though the technique was later applied more successfully to the plantation of Ulster. Law and order were gradually introduced in the southern Hebrides in 1605–15, and in the same decade Orkney and Shetland were permanently annexed to the Scottish crown.

▲ *Shetland Castle, built in 1600*

Victory over the Church

JAMES BECAME determined to bring the Scottish Church under his firm control. As King James I, he was also the head of the Church of England, and he lost no time in extending Anglican episcopacy to Scotland.

BETWEEN 1604 AND 1612 he exerted his powers and authority to institute bishops and dioceses. In 1606, a pliant Scottish parliament passed an act acknowledging the King's authority over all estates, secular or ecclesiastical. Having outmanoeuvred Melville and his colleagues, James gained control over the General Assembly which, in 1610, approved an episcopal constitution provided bishops were subject to the Assembly. Parliament ratified episcopacy in 1612 without this safeguard. Henceforward the bishops would be consecrated according to the Anglican rites and controlled only by a Court of High Commission as in England. The Assembly was last convened in 1618, and then only to sanction the ritual innovations known as the Five Articles of Perth. Though these changes soon became a dead letter, they were a source of friction for the future.

The expression 'Great Britain' began to be used in this period (and actually appeared in its abbreviated Latin form on English coins from 1604), but James's ambition to bring political union to the kingdoms was thwarted by both Scottish and English parliaments. The English were prejudiced against a people they considered uncivilised, they had no wish to merge their identity with what they considered an inferior nation, let alone

one that had been allied to Spain and
France. English markets were
not opened to Scottish
goods, or vice versa,
although inevitably
there was a gradual
improvement in
trade between the
two countries.

◄ *James VI of
Scotland, James I of
England*

Laud's Liturgy

CHARLES I, who had been born in Edinburgh in 1600, succeeded his father in March 1625. At first he followed the cautious policy of James with regard to the Scottish Church, giving way when he ran into strenuous opposition, especially over the Articles of Perth, although he negated this by the Act of Revocation which, by annexing all the Church lands alienated since 1542, drove the nobility into the Presbyterian camp.

THE NEW KING was born a Scot, but had very little understanding of Scottish affairs and even less of prevailing Scottish opinion. He knew nothing at all about the Highlands and not enough about the Lowlands. In 1633, for the first time, he came north for his Scottish coronation and foolishly persuaded parliament to pass an act insisting that the ministers wear white surplices instead of the black Genevan gown. The Book of Canons (1635) rationalised the lower levels of church administration, hitherto carried out by the presbyteries, and brought the Scottish Church into line with the Church of England in ritual matters. The service book devised by John Knox was replaced in 1637 by an Anglican prayer book (Laud's Liturgy) and the Scottish practice of extempore prayer was declared illegal.

On Sunday 23 July 1637, a riot erupted in St Giles Cathedral when the Dean began reading from the new prayer book. 'Traitor!' cried Jenny Geddes, hurling her stool at the Dean. 'Dost thou say Mass at my lug.' When Archbisop Spottiswoode tried to calm the congregation he was chased to his residence in a hail of stones. The alienation of the nobility was compounded by the resentment of the burgesses who had been taxed heavily to pay for the bishopric of Edinburgh.

▲ *Charles I*

The National Covenant, 1638

HAD CHARLES heeded the advice of his Privy Council and ordered the immediate withdrawal of Laud's Liturgy, the dangerous situation might have been defused; but obstinately he refused to give way and demanded the punishment of the ringleaders.

WHEN RIOTING occurred again on 18 October, Charles's answer was simply to punish those who refused to obey his orders concerning the use of the new prayer book. He ordered the removal of the Privy Council from Edinburgh to Linlithgow. Designed to bring the capital to heel, this measure had the opposite effect. The power vacuum in Edinburgh was filled by the establishment of Tables (four-man committees) which became the effective government of Scotland. The Tables drew up a Supplication or petition which demanded the recall of the new prayer book and the removal of the bishops from the Council.

Completely unwilling to compromise his position on the Church, Charles retaliated, on 19 February 1638, with a proclamation that denounced the Supplication as treason. The Four Tables, headed by the Earl of Home and Lord Lindsay, and with the nation united behind them, drew up the National League and Covenant based on the covenant of James VI in 1581. What James had had a hand in his son could not well reject. The Covenant was subscribed to by the great mass of the people of all ranks, beginning with a great ceremony in Greyfriars kirkyard, Edinburgh.

Greyfriars kirkyard, Edinburgh ▶

In the face of such solidarity Charles at length backed down, offering to withdraw the prayer book and restore a free Assembly, but it was now too little and too late.

The Bishops' Wars, 1639–41

THE ASSEMBLY, packed with extreme Presbyterians now known as Covenanters, met at Glasgow in December, refused to recognise Charles's commissioner, deposed the bishops and repealed all the acts of previous assemblies whereby episcopacy had been set up.

KING AND COVENANT were now on a collision course. The Covenanters acted promptly, raising two armies, one to defend the Borders and the other to coerce the north-east where episcopacy had its stronghold. In contrast to the poorly prepared, poorly led and poorly motivated armies of the English King, the Scots had the advantage of battle-hardened soldiers who had been serving in the Thirty Years' War under experienced generals like Alexander Leslie. Meanwhile, Charles planned to lead an army of 30,000, send a fleet to the Forth and recruit Irish troops to pillage Argyll. In June 1639, Charles and the Covenanters met near

◄ *Charles I*

Berwick. Hostilities were narrowly averted and a joint commission appointed to resolve grievances. Charles agreed to refer all disputed questions to the General Assembly or to parliament.

▲ *Berwick Upon Tweed today*

Charles was forced to summon the so-called Short Parliament in 1640, his first in 11 years. The Scots realised that the King had more to fear from an English parliament, and bided their time. When Charles dragged his heels, Leslie and the Earl of Montrose invaded England in August 1640 and occupied Newcastle. When the Scottish commissioners went to London to negotiate with the Long Parliament, they joined forces with the House of Commons. Charles visited Scotland in August 1641, gave way on all counts and tried to create a royalist party led by Montrose, now elevated to Marquis.

The Solemn League and Covenant, 1642

BY THE TREATY OF RIPON (October 1640), the quarrel between Charles and the Scots seemed to be patched up. Unfortunately for the King, some of the leading Scottish ministers, who had gone to London as commissioners under the terms of the peace treaty, were impressed by the Puritan atmosphere at Westminster. They formed the Assembly of Divines which aimed at 'a reformation in church discipline and ceremonies'. Effectively these Parliamentarians planned to establish Presbyterianism in both countries.

IN JUNE 1643, a Convention of the Estates met in Edinburgh and resolved to throw in its lot with the English Parliamentarians. On 2 August, the General Assembly met and drew up a pact of mutual defence which formed the basis of an alliance with the English parliament. This agreement was known as the Solemn League and Covenant, and it was essentially religious in content. The Parliamentarians had rebelled against the King on grounds of civil liberties, and had no great enthusiasm for the religious zealotry offered by the Scots, but for the time being they were in no position to argue

terms. On 25 September, they formally accepted the Covenant with only minor modifications.

The document set out its principal aim as 'the reformation of religion in the British Isles according to the word of God'. In return, the Scots undertook to raise an army of 18,000 infantry, 2,000 cavalry, 1,000 dragoons and a train of artillery, the English to pay £30,000 a month for its maintenance.

▲ *The Houses of Parliament, at Westminster – once renowned for their staunch Puritan atmosphere*

The Scots in the English Civil War

ON 19 JANUARY 1644, the Scottish army under Leslie (now Earl of Leven) crossed the Tweed. It would remain in England for the next three years and play a notable part in the war, as well as a crucial role in its outcome.

ALTHOUGH THE NORTHERN ENGLISH counties were held for the King by forces under the Marquis of Newcastle, Leven forced them to retreat to Marston Moor, where the Scots under Leven's nephew David Leslie were crucial to the Parliamentary victory on 2 July. Before the year was out, the Scots had helped to clear the north of England of Royalist forces. Oliver Cromwell's once-untutored army had now become the well-trained, well-armed New Model Army, also known as the 'Roundheads'.

Meanwhile, after a false start, Montrose launched his Royalist campaign. Aided by an Irish contingent he defeated Covenanting levies at Tippermuir and Aberdeen in September 1644 before turning to Argyll, whose Earl he savagely defeated at Inverlochy on 2 February 1645, with the help of the Macleans and the Macdonalds. Raw levies commanded by inexperienced generals hampered by meddling war committees, proved no match for Montrose in battles at Auldearn, Alford and Kilsyth, and his Highland hordes rampaged over northern Scotland at will. Glasgow surrendered and Edinburgh was at his mercy.

After the Royalists were beaten at Naseby in June, Leven's troops were recalled to combat the menace of Montrose, who was defeated at

Philiphaugh on 13 September 1645. So detested had Montrose's army become that Leslie's men took no prisoners. Even the female camp-followers were put to the sword. Both sides resorted to savagery unparalleled since the Dark Ages.

▲ *Charles I was desperate to keep the the Earl of Leven out of England*

Agreement between the Scots and Charles I

AFTER PHILIPHAUGH, the King's cause was hopeless. Although Montrose was still at large, the opposition of David Leslie and the Earl of Huntly effectively curbed him. By October 1645, Scotland was safe enough for the Covenanting army to return to England.

WHILE THE COVENANTERS exacted retribution from prominent Royalists, notably David Dickson (once Moderator of the General Assembly) and Robert Spottiswoode (once President of the Court of Session), David Leslie found that the Parliamentarians, having beaten the Royalists at Naseby, were no longer dependent on Scottish aid. The Independents, led by Oliver Cromwell, resented the Presbyterians with their doctrine of religious absolutism, and the Scots were no longer welcome in England.

Sensing deep division in the ranks of his enemies, Charles surrendered to the Scots at Southwell near Newark on 5 May 1646. The Scots withdrew to Newcastle, whence they began to bargain

Charles I ▶

with the King, offering him their support if he would accept the Covenant. Then the King and the Scots would unite against the English. Charles refused to abandon Anglicanism and the Cavaliers who had aided him, so the Scots surrendered him to the Parliamentary forces in exchange for a partial settlement of arrears in pay. By now real power in England had passed to Cromwell's New Model Army, at odds with the Scots. Imprisoned at Carisbrooke, Charles exploited the situation, intriguing with the Scots who offered military aid in exchange for his promise to establish Presbyterianism in England and suppress the Independents.

▲ *David Leslie, General of the Scots Army*

Preston, 1648

THE ENGAGEMENT of 27 December 1647 between Charles and the Scots was ratified by parliament in Edinburgh in March 1648. An ultimatum was sent to the English parliament on 11 April, demanding the King's release, the disbandment of the New Model Army and the establishment of Presbyterianism according to the Solemn League and Covenant.

A LARGE SECTION OF the Covenanting clergy were suspicious of the King's sincerity and outraged at the terms of the Engagement, which stipulated that Presbyterianism would be tried for only three years in England. This matter split the movement into Engagers and Anti-Engagers, leaving a legacy of bitterness for many years. An uprising by the latter faction was brutally crushed at Mauchline Moor.

In accordance with the Engagement, a Scottish army led by the Duke of Hamilton invaded England. It was poorly equipped, raw and undisciplined, and had little motivation for the King's cause. Not surprisingly, when it encountered Cromwell's army at Preston, Wigan and Warrington on 17–19 August it was decimated. Hamilton surrendered at Uttoxeter a week later, and was then executed while his followers dispersed.

In the aftermath of this disastrous campaign the General Assembly overruled parliament; the Anti-Engagers, led by the Marquis of Argyll, negotiated a settlement with Cromwell, who visited Edinburgh in October to receive a hero's welcome. By the Act of Classes, the Engagers were lumped together with Royalists and barred from holding any civil or military office.

▲ *Oliver Cromwell, Lord Protector of England 1653–58*

Charles II Lands in Scotland

THE EXECUTION OF CHARLES I in January 1649 antagonised the Scots. Cromwell's welcome was suddenly dulled – Charles had, after all, been King of their country too, and regicide was still an act against God. The Scots therefore proclaimed as king his son, Charles II, in defiance of the English Commonwealth.

THE SCOTS WOULD NOT receive the new King or grant him royal powers, however, until he signed the Solemn League and the National Covenant. Charles delayed for some time, but the failure of a Royalist uprising in April 1650, led by Montrose, who was captured and executed on 21 May, helped the King to make up his mind.

On 23 June, Charles sailed into the Spey estuary, and before going ashore signed the Covenants. From the outset, however, Charles was virtually a prisoner of the Anti-Engaging faction led by Argyll and the Earl of Loudoun. They faced considerable opposition on three fronts: discontented Royalists, the Engagers and other disgruntled elements among the Covenanters, and of course England. The Royalist threat was met by promptly expelling the King's entourage. Levies were hastily mobilised to meet the threat of English invasion. Scotland was now more deeply divided than ever.

During this critical period, Charles was segregated from the army that ostensibly fought for his cause and his humiliation was compounded by being forced to sign a document on 16 August, denouncing his father. Charles swallowed his pride but never forgave this insult.

Meanwhile, commissioners were appointed by parliament to root out 'Malignancy' in the ranks of the army. About 4,000 men were purged and the army irrevocably weakened.

▲ *Charles II returning from exile*

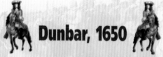

Dunbar, 1650

EVEN AFTER THESE PURGES, Leslie's army still numbered about 22,000 men, but they were inexperienced and lacking in officers. Opposing them was Cromwell's army of 5,000 horse and 11,000 foot.

THE OPENING ROUND was fought on ideological ground. Cromwell issued a declaration at the Border, calling on all 'God's elect' to join hands with their English brothers. The Scots, however, had been told to expect the worst atrocities at the hands of Cromwell's men, and resisted the invasion as stubbornly as any in the time of their forefathers.

On 28 July, Cromwell reached Musselburgh on the outskirts of Edinburgh, aiming to capture Leith where his fleet could be based, but

Leslie skilfully defended the port. The English were forced to retreat to Dunbar to replenish their stores. Successive attempts to attack Edinburgh and its environs were repulsed in August and Cromwell was forced to retreat to Dunbar once more. In one month he lost 5,000 men, mainly through disease and starvation.

The demoralised English appeared to be trapped when Leslie's army caught up with them on 1 September. Incredibly (and to Cromwell's delight) the Scots abandoned their strong positions and launched an attack on the night of 2–3 September. The English counter-attacked before dawn, and now it was the Scots who were trapped between the Brock Burn and a steep hill. Hungry, soaked to the skin, and poorly led, they were no match for Cromwell's disciplined troops. Defeat turned to a bloody rout in which about 3,000 were killed and 10,000 captured.

▼ *Cromwell and his troops at Dunbar*

Scotland Under Military Occupation, 1651–60

CROMWELL'S victory destroyed the unity of the Covenanting movement. The extremists drew up a Remonstrance blaming Argyll's government and rejecting the King, whose household was purged on 27 September. Argyll tried to steer an uneasy course between the Resolutioners and the Remonstrants.

I N RETALIATION, CHARLES himself broke free from the restraints imposed on him. At Strathbogie, in November 1650, an accommodation was reached between Royalists and the moderate Covenanters, as a result of which Charles was solemnly crowned at Scone on 1 January 1651, the Marquis of Argyll placing the crown on his head. When the Scottish parliament reconvened in May 1651, the Act of Classes was repealed by a series of resolutions which created a fresh breach between Resolutioners and Remonstrants.

Meanwhile, Cromwell's army remained in control of much of Scotland but Charles took the bold decision to invade England. On 31 July, the Scottish army headed south, in the vain hope of rallying English Royalists; but at Worcester on 3 September – exactly a year since the debacle at Dunbar – Cromwell defeated the Scots at Worcester. Charles fled abroad. The Scots were left at Cromwell's mercy, who set up an efficient system of government in both countries.

Scotland was effectively under military occupation for nine years, although the severity of this was mitigated by admitting Scotland to the United Commonwealth (which included Ireland). The Treaty also abol-

ished the monarchy. General Monck ruled Scotland efficiently and fairly, but Scotland was now too impoverished to benefit from free trade with England and her colonies.

Charles II ▶

The Restoration

AT THE REQUEST of General Monck, Charles II came back to reclaim his throne. Scotland played no part in the Restoration of Charles II, who promised to preserve the Church of Scotland, whose Covenants he had previously signed. But religion soon became the dominant, and divisive, issue of this reign.

I N MARCH 1661, the Scottish parliament passed the General Act Recissory, which repealed all legislation since 1633 and restored episcopacy. Bishops were appointed by the King and lay patronage (abolished in 1648) was restored. Holders of public offices were compelled to renounce the Covenants, and soon there were severe penalties for non-compliance and non-attendance at church. The country was ruled by royal commissioners, Middleton and Rothes, under whom the bishops wielded enormous influence.

The Presbyterians who clung to the Covenants came to be known as Covenanters, holding their own religious services (conventicles) in the open air, usually on remote moors and hillsides, and conducted by ejected ministers who were now fugitives from the law. Dragoons scoured the countryside, arresting Covenanters and suppressing conventicles by force. In defence, the Covenanters armed themselves and this led inevitably to open revolt. It began in Dumfries on 15 November 1666, and spread rapidly throughout the south-west. About 3,000 men, poorly armed but desperate, marched towards Edinburgh but on 28 November they were narrowly defeated at Rullion Green by government troops under Sir Tam

Covenanters holding an illegal service ▶

Dalziel of the Binns. In the aftermath of the Pentland Rising retribution was swift; the ringleaders were executed and many others tortured, imprisoned or banished.

Drumclog and Bothwell Bridge, 1679

THE DUKE OF LAUDERDALE, royal commissioner from 1667 to 1679, was at first sympathetic to the Covenanters, but their obduracy led to savage repression which, in turn, provoked reprisal.

CHIEF INSTIGATOR of the repression was James Sharpe, Archbishop of St Andrews, who was murdered at Magus Moor on 3 May, 1679, by extremists. On 29 May, about 80 Covenanters demonstrated defiance of the King at Rutherglen and mustered an army which clashed with government troops under James Graham of Claverhouse at Drumclog on 1 June, and drove them off in disarray.

Encouraged by this victory, the Covenanters marched on Glasgow, gathering support as they went, but at Bothwell Bridge, on 22 June, they were confronted by the government army. Had they held the bridge, victory might have been theirs; but they were let down badly by their commander, Robert Hamilton of Preston, whose cowardly incompetence led them to abandon their strong position and they were decisively beaten by James, the Duke of Monmouth (an illegitimate son of the King). About 400 were killed and 1,200 taken prisoner.

Retribution was as cruel as that following the Pentland Rising. Five men were hanged at Magus Moor, but over 1,000 prisoners were escorted in chains to Edinburgh where Greyfriars kirkyard (scene of the ceremonial signing of the Covenant) was converted into a concentration camp. By the end of July, 400 men, who had given their bond, were released, but the rest were shipped off to Barbados in November. Many of them drowned when the ship transporting them was wrecked in Orkney.

Orkney, where many prisoners were drowned en route to Barbados ▶

The Killing Time, 1680–88

TO DEFUSE the situation, Monmouth treated the rebels lightly, but was soon replaced by his uncle, the Duke of York (later James VII and II) who, in spite of his own tolerant attitude, presided over a period of terror which came to be known as the Killing Time.

JAMES, HIMSELF A secret Catholic, was inclined towards tolerance and moderation, and he did his best to alleviate the situation by fostering trade and industry. Ironically, parliament now applied the penal laws, originally aimed at Catholics, to the Covenanters. The enforcement of the Test Act was so rigid that even the episcopal clergy revolted; many refused to take the Test and were ejected from their livings.

Repression was followed by conciliation, three Acts of Indulgence effectively splitting the Presbyterian ranks. The extremists centred round Donald Cargill and Richard Cameron and at Sanquhar on 22 June 1680, the anniversary of Bothwell Bridge, they proclaimed their defiance, disowning 'Charles Stewart' on grounds of perjury and breach of covenant. The Cameronians were massacred at Airds Moss a month later.

After James left Scotland in 1682, government-sponsored cruelty reached new levels, with arbitrary arrest, torture and deportation to the plantations of the West Indies commonplace. Bands of dragoons roamed the country at will, murdering or mutilating suspected Covenanters, raping, pillaging and burning. On account of these atrocities, Graham of Claverhouse, the chief agent of the Killing Time, was derisively known as 'Bluidy Clavers'.

In 1680, extremists gathered on the anniversary of Bothwell Bridge ▶

IN HONOUR

OF

THE COVENANTERS

WHO FOUGHT AND FELL IN THE

BATTLE OF BOTHWELL BRIDGE

22ND JUNE 1679

IN DEFENCE OF

CIVIL AND RELIGIOUS LIBERTY

ERECTED BY PUBLIC SUBSCRIPTION

1903

BOTHWELL BRIDGE

22ND JUNE 1679

James VII and II, 1685–88

WHEN JAMES succeeded his brother in 1685, he did not take the coronation oath which bound him to uphold Protestantism. Instead, he pushed through an Act of Indemnity, relieving Catholics of the worst burdens, but expressly excluding 'recusants', who were now terrorised more thoroughly than before.

ARCHIBALD, EARL OF ARGYLL (son of the Great Marquis) was in exile under sentence of death for refusing to take the Test, but he returned to Scotland and tried to raise a rebellion in conjunction with Monmouth. It was ill-timed, however, and soon collapsed – this resulted in Argyll being beheaded. Some 200 were tortured in Dunnottar Castle for two months before the majority were sent to the plantations.

After this rebellion, the government made attendance at a conventicle a hanging offence. While pursuing nonconformity so ruthlessly, the King could hardly secure a measure of greater toleration for Catholics. In the end, however, he overruled parliament and exercised his royal prerogative to accord complete toleration to all his subjects, Catholics, Covenanters and Quakers alike. The Declaration of Indulgence (1687) effectively brought the Killing Time to an end, but suspicion of the King's motives and the fear that Catholicism would be imposed failed to win over the majority of Scots. Opposition to the King grew rapidly, aided by Protestant forces in Holland, where his son-in-law, William of Orange, had his sights set on the throne of England and Scotland. In the events of 1688 which led to the flight of the King and the advent of the Prince of

Orange, Scotland played a relatively passive role. Not till William had been in England for a month did the Edinburgh mob sack Holyrood (which had been made a place of Catholic worship). Some episcopal clergy in the south-west were attacked but otherwise the country was calm.

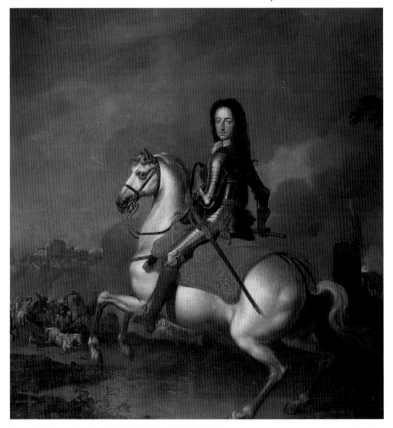

▲ *William of Orange*

Killiecrankie and Dunkeld, 1689

A MAJORITY OF THE Convention of Estates, called in April 1689, declared that James had forfeited the crown which was formally offered jointly to William and his wife Mary, and entailed on their issue and that of Mary's sister, Princess Anne.

B Y THE CLAIM OF RIGHT, the new monarchs recognised that episcopacy was unsupportable in Scotland and presbyterianism was restored. The Church of Scotland was thus re-established by the Revolution. At the same time, however, supporters of episcopacy (which was strong in the north-east) became the nucleus of a Jacobite party. James Graham of Claverhouse, whom James VII had created Viscount Dundee, stormed out of the Convention, raised a force which held Edinburgh Castle for the deposed King, and subsequently organised an army, mainly of Highlanders, which advanced south into Perthshire, confronting the forces of the new government under General

▲ *William and Mary*

Hugh Mackay at Killiecrankie, a pass that controlled a vital road through the Highlands.

The headlong charge of the Highlanders unnerved the government soldiers, who were overwhelmed before they could fix their newfangled plug-bayonets. While the Highlanders were seizing their booty, the remnant of Mackay's forces escaped as night fell. It was some consolation that the Highlanders suffered heavy losses, including Dundee himself. The victory of Killiecrankie gave the Highlanders false hopes, for without Dundee in command, they failed to exploit that victory any further. A series of unsuccessful skirmishes ensued. The Williamite army fell back in good order, defeating a Jacobite force in Perth. At Dunkeld, on 21 August, an army of 5,000 Highlanders was defeated by the newly raised Cameronian Regiment of 1,200 men under its youthful colonel, William Cleland, who was killed in the hour of victory.

▼ *Viscount Dundee slain at Killiecrankie*

The Religious Settlement, 1690

THE DEATH OF DUNDEE, and the decisive defeat at Dunkeld, brought the war to an end, but several years elapsed before Scotland was truly at peace and the religious problems settled.

ALTHOUGH THE MAJORITY of the people wished to see presbyterianism restored, William was acutely aware of the antagonism of the Church of England (of which he was titular head) if he did not maintain support for episcopacy in Scotland. Fortunately, he had as his adviser William Carstairs, whom he had known in Holland, and through his wisdom and diplomacy a moderate form of presbyterianism was finally established. Patronage was abolished and the surviving ministers who had been ejected since 1661 were restored to their parishes. In October 1690, the General Assembly met for the first time since 1653.

Significantly, none of the 180 delegates came from the north-east, stronghold of episcopacy. At the other end of the spectrum, the three Cameronian ministers decided to conform to the new establishment. Although they had welcomed and enthusiastically supported the Revolution, the rank and file of the Cameronian movement were soon disenchanted with the new regime. Deserted by their own ministers, these extreme Presbyterians refused to take the oath of allegiance. Although it was not till 1706 that they were joined by two ministers, they became the nucleus of that dissent which, in the ensuing centuries, would lead to many breakaway movements from the Church of Scotland.

▲ *William Carstairs, who advised William of Orange on bringing Presbyterianism to Scotland*

The Massacre at Glencoe, 1692

THE FIRST OF the major crises to mar the reign of William and Mary concerned the pacification of the Highlands, where many of the clans remained sympathetic to James VII, now living in exile in France. Highlanders were still mostly Catholic, and found it hard to swear loyalty to an anti-Catholic, anti-Stuart, anti-French king who was not even English born.

FEAR OF A FRENCH invasion in support of the deposed king led the government to make payments to clan chiefs if they would take the oath of allegiance to William and Mary, 31 December 1691 was fixed as the deadline for submission. Alexander Macdonald of Glencoe made it a point of honour to delay until the last moment, but then made the mistake of presenting himself to an official who was not authorised to take his submission. He should have taken his oath to Inverness, not to Fort William as he did – it seems likely that he may have been deliberately misinformed as to where he should go. As a result, he did not swear allegiance till 6 January.

This minor bureaucratic slip was seized by the Under Secretary of State for Scotland, Sir John Dalrymple, Master of Stair, as the pretext to make an example. In the traditional manner, letters of fire and sword were issued against the Macdonalds with a view to dispersing this clan, as had happened to the MacGregors a century earlier, however the task was entrusted to troops under Campbell of Glenlyon. For two weeks the

Campbells enjoyed the hospitality of the Macdonalds, and then, during the night of 12–13 February, murdered about 40 of their hosts. Due to miscalculations on the part of the Campbells, the operation was bungled and many Macdonalds managed to escape. The atrocity aroused widespread indignation, even in the Lowlands, yet an enquiry was not held until 1695, as a result of which Dalrymple was dismissed. William's failure to deal swiftly with the matter intensified anti-English feeling.

▲ *Victim in the massacre of Glencoe*

The Darien Scheme, 1698–1700

WILLIAM PATERSON, who founded the Bank of England in 1694, devised a brilliant plan to revitalise the Scottish economy by establishing a colony on the isthmus of Darien in Panama, at the crossroads of Pacific and Atlantic trade.

PATERSON FORMED THE AFRICA and Indies Company, whose capital was fixed at £600,000, half from Scotland and the rest from England. Despite the fact that Darien was Spanish territory, the scheme was enthusiastically hailed by the Scots, but disappointment set in when the East India Company and certain English businessmen opposed it and forced the House of Commons to bar English shareholders. The Scots tried to raise the capital unaided; the share subscription was virtually a rerun of the National Covenant in 1638 as people of all ranks and professions flocked to pledge their cash. Late in 1698, the promoters despatched 1,000 settlers who found to their horror that Darien was infested with malaria. Two further contingents of colonists were sent out, but disease, famine and Spanish raids doomed the venture.

William himself withdrew his support in 1700 when negotiating the Partition Treaties with Spain. In March that year the colony was evacuated but its ships were wrecked by storms on the journey home and few survivors returned to Scotland. The failure of the Darien Scheme was the greatest commercial disaster in Scotland's history. Apart from the appalling loss of life, many thousands of investors lost their savings.

▲ *Greyfriars kirkyard, site of the ceremony of the National Covenant*

Proposals for Union, 1702–03

THE DISASTROUS failure of the Darien Scheme left such a legacy of bitterness towards England that it seemed doubtful whether the union of the crowns would be maintained. When William III died in March 1702, his sister-in-law Anne succeeded to both Scottish and English thrones, but as the last of her 18 children died young, there was a widespread feeling that, on her death, Scotland would terminate the union of the crowns.

I N FACT, THE SETTLEMENTS in both countries at the Revolution were so different that a continuation of the existing constitution became increasingly impracticable. Prior to the Revolution, the Scottish parliament was far less representative of the people than its English counterpart, and its organisation and procedures were easily manipulated by the government. Its powers were in the hands of a committee called the Lords of the Articles, selected by the government. This committee was abolished by the settlement of 1689 and William, as a constitutional monarch, found it increasingly difficult to impose his will on two separate parliaments.

The notion of a political union of the kingdoms was nothing new, and had been proposed by James VI and I almost as soon as he came to the English throne in 1603. Cromwell had ruled Scotland as part of his unified Commonwealth and the Scots had profited from the trading privileges this entailed, but the Restoration had swept them aside. When the Scots were barred from direct trading with England under the Navigation Act (1670), Charles II had proposed a union.

▲ *Queen Anne*

Act of Union, 1707

DARIEN was the catalyst which seemed to make union increasingly desirable. The Scots made no provision for the settlement of the crown after Anne's death and to forestall the likelihood of a Jacobite king succeeding her political union became imperative.

THE MERCHANT classes of Scotland, in the aftermath of Darien, perceived the commercial advantages that would accrue from union, but the English Whigs, drawn mostly from the merchant classes, strenuously opposed this and Scots of all classes were far less enthusiastic for union than they had been in 1689. In addition to the strong Tory-Jacobite faction, there was a Patriot or Country party, headed by Andrew Fletcher of Saltoun, which felt that the way ahead was a Scotland completely independent of England. Such was the impact of the Patriot and Jacobite combination in 1703–04 that relations with England deteriorated to a dangerously low level.

Ironically, it was the Whigs in the House of Commons who, going against the wishes and vested interests of their own supporters, began to push forward plans for union on the basis of freedom of trade and safeguards for the Church of Scotland, the Scottish courts of justice and Scots law. The Scottish Whigs agreed, and in April 1706 commissioners

The Act of Union being presented to Queen Anne ▶

from both countries began negotiating the details whereby Scotland would get 45 members in the Commons and 16 representative peers in the Lords. In January 1707, the proposed union was confirmed in the Scottish parliament by a majority of 110 to 68 and ratified by both parliaments. The Act of Union cemented what had been a growing interdependence between the two countries.

Rise of Jacobitism, 1708

THE ORDINARY PEOPLE of Scotland were decidedly hostile to the union from the outset and there was a general feeling that the Scottish commissioners – 'such a parcel of rogues in a nation' – had been bribed with English gold.

ONTROVERSY has surrounded this matter ever since; but whether bribery had carried the day or not, it left a feeling of resentment in which sympathy for the Jacobite cause began to increase. The first general election for the new British parliament (1708) effectively blessed the union, largely because of the fear raised by a French landing near Edinburgh in March, foiled at the last moment by the arrival of the Royal Navy.

The Jacobite faction, thwarted by the failure of the French invasion, tried to subvert the union by other means. The government imprisoned a number of known Jacobites, including the Duke of Gordon and the Earls of Moray, Seaforth and Traquair, and there was an outcry when they were transferred to the Tower of London to stand trial for high treason. In fact, they formed part of the Squadrone, an incongruous alliance with Godolphin and Marlborough, who were intriguing against their Whig colleagues to hedge their bets in the event of a Jacobite restoration.

Scots resentment was exacerbated by the introduction of the English tax system, but most of all by the grant of toleration to Scottish episcopalians and the reintroduction of lay patronage in 1712. By the time of Anne's death in 1714 – allowing George I, a Hanoverian

Queen Anne, who died in 1714 ▶

Lutheran, to become King of Great Britain and Ireland under the Act of Settlement – the party which had engineered the union had suffered most from its effects.

Hanoverian Accession: George I, 1714-27

THE ACCESSION OF George Louis, Elector of Hanover, as King George I was achieved peacefully, despite a suspicion that Anne's Tory ministers had favoured the Old Pretender (the son of James VII, now aged 26).

BORN IN 1660, George Louis was the son of Sophia, youngest daughter of Elizabeth, daughter of James VI and known as the Winter Queen of Bohemia. After the death of Queen Anne's only son to survive infancy, the next Protestant heir to the thrones of Scotland and England was Sophia. The Act of Settlement (1701) secured the inheritance to her and her descendants. Sophia died on 8 June 1714 and Queen Anne on 1 August, leaving the way clear to George Louis to succeed in both Hanover and the British Isles.

He inherited from his father the lay bishopric of Osnabruck and the duchy of Calenberg, while his marriage to his cousin Sophia Dorothea in 1682 brought him the duchy of Celle. George, derisively known to his Scottish subjects as 'the wee, wee German lairdie', never visited Scotland and regarded his British dominions merely as a means of improving his position in Germany. He was content to leave the business of government in the hands of his ministers, and it was in this reign that the office of prime minister, held by Robert Walpole from 1721 onwards, gradually developed.

James VI, great grandfather of George I ▶

The Jacobite Rebellions of 1715

THE GENERAL ELECTION early in 1715 brought the Whigs back to power with an increased majority, largely as a result of Protestant fears of Jacobitism in Scotland. Having failed to restore the Stuart dynasty by parliamentary means, the Jacobites took up arms.

THE UPRISING BEGAN in south-west England, but was quickly extinguished. In Scotland, rumours of an imminent uprising had been rife since May 1714, but it was not until 7 September 1715 that the Earl of Mar raised the Jacobite standard in the Highlands and north-east. James VIII and III was proclaimed at Aberdeen, and Mar's army advanced on Perth. The death of Louis XIV abruptly stopped French support, and instead of marching on Edinburgh, Mar delayed at Perth. Meanwhile, the government hurriedly passed 'an Act for encouraging loyalty in Scotland', popularly known as the Clan Act, the first step in the destruction of the traditional power of the clan chiefs and of the Highland landowners.

Mar's advance on Edinburgh was checked by government troops under the Duke of Argyll at Sheriffmuir near Dunblane on 13 November. Technically, the battle was a draw, but Mar was forced to retreat to Perth, failing to exploit his advantage against the heavily outnumbered Duke. A rising in northern England was broken the following day. The Old Pretender landed at Peterhead on 22 December, spent three weeks at Perth, and then fled with Mar and other Jacobite leaders. Fewer than 30 men were executed for treason but several hundred prisoners were transported to the American plantations. Many of them were tried at Carlisle, no Scottish jury being willing to convict them.

Louis XIV of France ▲

Wade's Military Roads

UNDER THE CLAN ACT, the estates of Jacobite nobles were forfeited and those tenants who had remained loyal to the crown were rewarded with two years remission of rents.

THE SALE OF FORFEITED estates caused a great deal of suffering and injustice, although the worst excesses were later mitigated by the Act of Indemnity (1717). Charles XII of Sweden, a long-time

enemy of George I, conspired with Spain and the Duke of Ormonde to mount a Jacobite invasion. The death of Charles on 11 December 1718 robbed the venture of its main source of arms and cash, but the invasion went ahead as planned. A Spanish Armada of 29 ships, carrying 5,000 troops and vast quantities of arms, left Cadiz on 7 March 1719, but, like its famous forebear, it came to grief in severe storms. A diversionary expedition of two frigates, 300 Spanish troops and a party of Jacobites under the Earl Marischal landed at Loch Duich on 13 April, but were defeated by government troops at Glenshiel on 10 June.

General George Wade, Commander-in-Chief of the army in Scotland, prepared a report on the state of the Highlands and made recommendations to bring this troublesome area into line with the rest of the country. An Act for Disarming the Highlands was passed in 1725, but was ineffectual as the weapons surrendered were all antiques of little military value. Wade was infinitely more successful in his construction of a network of military roads through the Highlands (1725–36), 500 soldiers being employed each summer in laying tracks and building bridges, many of which survive to this day.

◀ *A Wade bridge: Garva Bridge over the Spey*

The Highland Forts

NOT SINCE the time of Lollius Urbicus had there been such an ambitious project of military engineering in Scotland.

WHERE THE TERRAIN permitted, Wade's roads ran in straight lines, Roman fashion, with a standard width of 5 m (16 ft). Altogether, some 400 km (250 miles) of roads were constructed, as well as 40 bridges. These roads considerably stimulated trade, although their primary objective was to make the policing of the Highlands easier.

The roads linked a series of great military fortifications. Forts George, Augustus and William were erected on the Castle Hill at Inverness, at the southern end of Loch Ness and at the head of Loch Linnhe respectively, thus forming a defensive chain along the Great Glen, while Ruthven Barracks was erected on a hill between Kingussie and Aviemore. Fort William, named after William III, had originated as an earth-and-wattle fort built by General Monck in 1655, later rebuilt in stone. Fort Augustus was named after the Hanoverian prince, Augustus, Duke of Cumberland.

Ironically, these fortresses proved powerless to keep the Highlanders in check when they next rose in support of 'the King over the water'. All three were demolished by the Jacobites, who made their last stand at Ruthven in 1746. The last vestiges of Fort William vanished in 1864 when the railway was built, while the picturesque ruins of Fort Augustus are now part of the Benedictine Abbey (1878). A new Fort George was erected (1748–63) near Ardersier. Only Ruthven Barracks remains as a romantic reminder of the Jacobite rebellions.

Fort George today ▶

The Black Watch

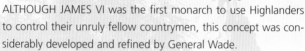

ALTHOUGH JAMES VI was the first monarch to use Highlanders to control their unruly fellow countrymen, this concept was considerably developed and refined by General Wade.

T O ASSIST IN THE decommissioning of Jacobite weapons, in 1729 he raised a Highland gendarmerie known as the Black Watch (*Am Freiceadan Dubh*) from the dark tartan of their kilts, in contrast with the Redcoats (*An Arm Dearg*) of the regular army who wore scarlet tunics and breeches. Initially recruited from clans that had proved their loyalty to William of Orange and later to George I, the Black Watch was gradually expanded to include men from all parts of the Highlands, although they were often ostracised by their own families and were obliged to serve in other districts. Their patrols proved very effective in watching rival clans and preventing raids and reprisals.

By 1730 there were six companies, officered by Highland chiefs who had proved their loyalty, and in 1739 the force was expanded and formed into a line regiment as

The Black Watch Monument at Aberfeldy ▶

the 43rd Foot. In 1751 they became the 42nd Foot, or Highland, Regiment but later reverted to the original name as the Black Watch (Royal Highlanders).

What had started as a police force would become the first of many Highland regiments in the service of the British Empire, and the battle honours of the 'Gallant Forty-Twa' range from the Seven Years' War (1756–63) to the Korean War.

George II, 1727-60

THE ACCESSION of George II in 1727 had little or no impact on the conduct of affairs in Scotland. The new monarch retained his father's ministry and the parliament which met in 1728 had an even larger Whig majority than before.

IN SCOTLAND, the government party were nicknamed the Argathelians, from their leader, the Duke of Argyll. Their opponents, both Tory and Jacobite, were known as the Squadrone.

During the long premiership of Horace Walpole (1721–42), the gradual improvement in trade and industry began to reconcile the Scots to the union with England, but from time to time government measures roused fierce antagonism.

A malt tax, introduced in 1707, was so strenuously resisted that it was not till 1725 that Walpole attempted to enforce it. This was met by ferocious riots in Glasgow when Wade sent troops to protect the excisemen, and the mansion of Daniel Campbell of Shawfield, the Glasgow MP, was demolished. Typically, Edinburgh reacted differently to the hated tax; there the brewers merely went on strike. After a week without beer, however, the Scots were forced to give way and paid the tax.

In 1733, Walpole introduced a new Excise Bill, a measure that united his enemies as never before. Former allies, such as the Duke of Montrose (Lord Privy Seal) and the Earl of Stair (Vice Admiral) changed sides and were promptly stripped of their offices.

George II when he was Prince of Wales ▶

The Porteous Riots, 1736

FISCAL MEASURES imposed on Scotland in defiance of the Act of Union did little to endear the Scots to Westminster government. At grass roots level this was manifest in a universal disregard for the duties on tea, wine and spirits. As a result, the smuggling of these commodities attained the level of a national industry.

T HE ONLY OPPONENTS of this illicit trade were the citizens of the royal burghs (who enjoyed the privilege of importing such foreign goods) and the General Assembly (which regarded the consumption of such stimulants as sinful).

In 1736, two smugglers, Robertson and Wilson, were sentenced to death for robbing a collector of customs. On the eve of their execution they tried to escape from the Edinburgh Tolbooth. Robertson got away; Wilson, unable to follow, at least prevented the guards from catching his friend. To the general public, Wilson was a hero and a martyr, and the authorities redoubled their efforts to ensure that his execution was carried out. On 14 April, Wilson was escorted to the gallows by the City Guard commanded by Captain Porteous.

▼ *Westminster's harsh measures led to a huge increase in smuggling*

Immediately after Wilson was hanged the mob went berserk and the Guard discharged a volley, killing several people. Porteous was tried and sentenced to death but Queen Caroline (acting as regent) ordered a six-week stay of execution. Believing that Porteous was to be reprieved, the mob took justice into their own hands, stormed the Tolbooth on 7 September and hanged him from a dyer's pole. There was no fuss, and the vigilantes were never brought to book.

▼ *Porteous is hanged by the mob*

Bonnie Prince Charlie

THE JACOBITE movement had been quiescent for years when it suddenly sprang to life again, thanks to the energy, drive and charisma of Prince Charles Edward Stuart, son of the Old Pretender and grandson of James VII and II.

THE JACOBITE cause was always powerful enough to be considered the greatest threat to Britain, and the outbreak of war in 1743 between Britain and France provided the exiled Jacobites with the opportunity to stage another rebellion. French troops were mustered for an invasion in February 1744, but their ships were wrecked in a storm. Impatiently, Prince Charles went ahead with his plans anyway. Sailing from Nantes aboard the *Doutelle* with 'the seven men of Moidart', Charles landed on Eriskay in the Outer Hebrides on 23 July 1745 while George II was away in Hanover. French ships joined him with supplies and artillery.

There was little enthusiasm for this rash venture, and it says much for the Prince's personal magnetism that he overcame the doubters and eventually rallied such a formidable army to his cause. Despite a rebuff from Macdonald of Boisdale, he crossed to the mainland, landing at Borrodale near Arisaig on 25 July. Again his reception was cool, but he won over Macdonald of Clanranald, Cameron of Lochiel and Macdonnell of Glengarry. Between them they had over 1,000 men. At Glenfinnan, on 19 August, the standard of James VIII was raised.

Though he never had as many men as Mar in 1715, Charles had luck,

daring and the incompetence of his enemy on his side. After some victo-
rious skirmishes, his army entered Edinburgh unopposed (aided by the
Provosts who secretly left the gates open) and Charles as Regent of the
three kingdoms took up residence at Holyrood.

▲ *Bonnie Prince Charlie*

Falkirk and Culloden, 1745–46

THE JACOBITE and Hanoverian forces clashed at Prestonpans on 21 September, where Charles's soldiers employed their broadswords in the famous Highland charge. Under Sir John Cope, the Hanoverian forces were soundly defeated. Charles waited at Edinburgh in the hope of winning greater support, but when this was not forthcoming he set off on the march south to London, hoping to rally support along the way.

THE JACOBITE army crossed the Border on 9 November and got as far as Derby on 4 December. By that time regiments had been recalled from the Continent and formed two armies, under the Duke of Cumberland and Marshal Wade respectively. As these forces converged on Derby, Charles reluctantly agreed on a tactical withdrawal via Carlisle and Dumfries to Glasgow and Stirling, where he besieged the castle.

On 17 January 1746, the Jacobites attacked General Hawley's relieving column at Falkirk and won their second (and last) victory. Despite this success, Charles failed to win over the Lowlands and withdrew into the Highlands, taking Fort Augustus and Inverness whither he hoped a French expedition would provide reinforcements. Help never materialised, and the Jacobites made their last stand on Culloden Moor on 17 April. The

Duke of Cumberland, George II's youngest son, was Commander-in-Chief of British forces on the Continent. He had sent over 10 of his best battalions, supported by a contingent of Dutch troops. The 5,000 Jacobites, therefore, were no match for the government troops – almost twice their number and better trained and equipped. About 1,000 Jacobites were killed in the battle but many more were slaughtered by dragoons pursuing them.

Charles himself escaped, to become 'the Prince in the heather' of Highland romance. After many adventures in the Highlands and Islands he escaped to France in September.

▼ *'The son of your king has come to ask for a little bread'*

Aftermath of Rebellion

COMPARED WITH the leniency towards prisoners in 1715, the government reaction in 1746 was savage. Apart from the rebels who were given no quarter, earning for Cumberland his nickname of 'the Butcher', about 80 prisoners were executed and many others were transported to the plantations of America and the West Indies.

THE LAST JACOBITE rebellion did more harm than good for the Highlanders: the Scottish clans became regarded as nothing more than barbarians, leading to the passing of a new Disarming Act. Under the terms of this Act, Highlanders were forbidden to wear their traditional tartan. The bagpipes were deemed to be an instrument of war and were likewise banned under penalties of a heavy fine in the first instance or transportation to the colonies for repeated infringement. Government officials were given the power to search houses at will. These draconian measures were not repealed till 1782. Because of their prominent role in the late uprising, the Episcopalians of the north-east (unless they were members of the Church of England) were similarly penalised until 1792.

One of the few positive measures was the abolition of hereditary jurisdictions (1747), a reform of a system that was open to corruption and abuse. There was something inherently unjust and inefficient in a system that permitted bailies and magistrates to inherit their positions and hold them for life. Holders of such hereditary judgeships were well compensated, however, and as many of them used the money to effect agricultural improvements, Scotland as a whole benefited.

◀ *Tartan and bagpipes were banned under the Disarming Act*

The Destruction of the Clan System

FOUR TIMES in little more than half a century, the peace of Scotland was severely disrupted by a rebellion which had begun in the Highlands and was largely made possible by the chiefs who were able to mobilise their clansmen under a feudal system that had not altered for centuries.

DESPITE THE MEASURES taken to disarm the Highlands (which, paradoxically, had left the loyal clans helpless) – the erection of forts, the construction of military roads and the Black Watch – the rebellion of 1745–46 had proved much more dangerous than Mar's rebellion of 1715. Clearly, the clan system itself was the root cause of the trouble, and now the government moved to destroy it for ever.

The Highland chief derived his authority from the principle of clanship, the ties of blood and family which had proved far stronger than feudalism or any modern relationship between landowner and tenant. The ancient system of land tenure known as wardholding was abolished.

Hitherto the chief held the clan land as virtual head of an extended family. Now he became owner of the land, and his clansmen, who had hitherto enjoyed their land in exchange for personal or military service, became merely his tenants, paying rent.

▲ *Garva Bridge, part of an important military road built at this time*

It was this inexorable advance of a money economy into the Highlands, and not the effects of any royal statute, that finally ended the supremacy of the clans. For a generation, the age-old concepts of chief and clan continued, but the ancient traditions of loyalty and kinship were gradually eroded. In due course the destruction of the clan system would drastically alter the economic character of the Highlands and leave a legacy of bitterness to this day.

▼ *Clan chieftains had great authority*

The Highland Regiments

THE GREAT CIVIL WAR in the middle of the eighteenth century brought to an abrupt end centuries of a way of life known as Celtic, and imposed on the Highlands a British social system. The loyalty of clans such as the Campbells, Mackays and Mackenzies during the rebellion, meanwhile, was eventually rewarded by the raising of Highland regiments for service in the British army.

THIS WAS PROPOSED by Duncan Forbes of Culloden, Lord Advocate and President of the Court of Session, as far back as 1738. A major Highland landowner himself, he had an intimate knowledge of the Highlands and their people. He estimated that a force of 5,000 men could be raised for overseas service, officered by their clan chiefs and organised into clan regiments. Thus the warlike propensities of the Highlander could be turned to practical advantage, and a source of rebellion strictly controlled.

Had this recommendation of Forbes been accepted earlier, the rebellion might have been nipped in the bud, but, though Walpole endorsed this plan, English antipathy towards a standing army and the Scottish Lowlander's fear of another Highland Host aborted the scheme. When the Black Watch became a line regiment in 1739, it was expressly for service in Scotland. In 1743, it was ordered to London and inspected by Wade at Finchley, but Jacobite agents told the men that they were being sent to the West Indies. They decamped for the north, but were apprehended near Oundle, brought back to London, found guilty of mutiny and sentenced

Seaforth Highlanders, in nineteenth-century uniform ▶

to death. In fact only two NCOs and a private were shot, the rest being scattered among regiments then serving overseas.

Despite this bad beginning, between 1740 and 1815 alone more than 50 battalions of Highlanders fought in all Britain's wars with incomparable distinction.

Industrial Progress

WITH A FEW minor exceptions, the peace of Scotland was not disturbed after 1746. In the ensuing period of peace and stability, enormous progress was achieved in industry and commerce, agriculture and fishing.

N THE FIELD OF textiles, the manufacture of linen increased sixfold between 1728 and 1771. Aided by grants of assistance from the British Linen Company, linen became Scotland's chief export, dominating the Scottish economy for a century. The Irvine Valley became a major centre for lace production; Edinburgh, Haddington and Musselburgh were the leading woollen towns; Kilmarnock made its name initially for bonnets but soon diversified into carpets; hosiery became the speciality of the north-east; while Dunfermline, Dundee and Stonehaven concentrated on weaving and Stirling emerged as the centre for blankets, serges and tartan cloth. Hawick was the first of the Border towns to develop a woollen industry. Glasgow, meanwhile, began a period of phenomenal growth, fuelled enormously by the flourishing tobacco trade with the American colonies, followed by cotton and sugar from the West Indies.

With its rich deposits of iron and coal, Scotland was well-placed to benefit from the Industrial Revolution. The Carron Ironworks was established in 1760 and rapidly became the wonder of the age. With 1,200 workers, it was by far the largest factory of its kind anywhere in Europe. The textile industry might profit from the inventions of Arkwright and Compton, but through the genius of James Watt and William Symington it was Scotland that launched the Age of Steam.

▲ *James Watt's steam engine*

Agricultural Improvements

THE CASH PAID in compensation for the abolition of hereditary jurisdictions was wisely invested by landowners in a variety of agricultural improvements.

THIS MOVEMENT began with the abandonment of the age-old run-rig system, whereby the alternate ridges of a field were in the hands of different farmers. The removal of this barrier was accompanied by the use of more efficient ploughs, the introduction of field drainage, the clearing of ditches and hedgerows, and the planting of trees as windbreaks.

At the same time, the study of soil chemistry led to improved methods of liming and fertilising, as well as the practice of crop rotation. New crops were imported and improved strains of existing plants were introduced. In particular the turnip, used as winter feed, obviated the need to kill off cattle at the onset of winter.

These improvements went hand in hand with the adoption of farm machinery and equipment, ranging from mechanical drills to threshing machines. The light plough with steel coulter drawn by two horses replaced the heavy wooden ploughs drawn by teams of oxen.

The greater prosperity of Scotland was reflected in the construction of public works. Thomas Telford was a man of bridge- and road-building genius, whose enormous influence on the Industrial Revolution throughout Britain also helped transform his country, and the world. Alongside the Roman wall which had once divided the country there now ran the Forth and Clyde Canal, engineered between 1768 and 1790 at a cost of £300,000. In the same period the Clyde was deepened and communications improved by new bridges at Glasgow, Dumfries, Perth and Edinburgh.

◄ *Horses began to replace oxen on farms*

Social Changes

ALTHOUGH the peasantry of Scotland were not tied to the land as they were in many European countries, a form of serfdom survived in regard to colliers and saltworkers.

STILL SEEKING TO destroy the powerful clans, the government in London aimed to break the link between the chief and the rest of his clan by reducing the chief to the role of land proprietor. Clansmen became workers. They were bound, from birth, to the works with which their families were connected, and could be bought and sold by their masters at will. If a freeman became a collier he lost his freedom after a year. Severe penalties were enforced on runaways or those who harboured them. This pernicious system was abolished by an Act of 1775, not for humanitarian but for purely economic reasons. The demand from burgeoning industry for coal and salt was now greater than the supply and under the existing conditions it was impossible to recruit an increased workforce. The Act stipulated that henceforward people who voluntarily became colliers or saltworkers would no longer forfeit their liberty, while those born in servitude would be liberated after a term of years proportionate to the age they had reached at the passing of the Act. Thus it was not until 1799 that the last vestiges of industrial serfdom disappeared.

Attempts by the government to remove some of the disabilities imposed on Catholics by William III provoked rioting in Glasgow and Edinburgh, and were strenuously rejected by the General Assembly (May 1778), articulating the fear and hatred of Rome which remained intense in Scotland. The measure passed in England, although the Gordon riots (1780) showed that religious bigotry was just as deep-rooted there.

▲ *William III, a fervent anti-Catholic monarch*

Henry Dundas, 1775-1801

HENRY DUNDAS, appointed Lord Advocate in 1775, was for almost three decades the government's chief agent in Scotland. In time, his power became so absolute that he was nicknamed Henry IX, the uncrowned King of Scots.

HE HAD MANY admirable personal qualities, and in the political arena he was genial to friend and foe alike. He came from a powerful family which had furnished two Lords President (his father and brother) as well as other judges. Even his Whig opponents grudgingly conceded that he was the right man for Scotland at the time.

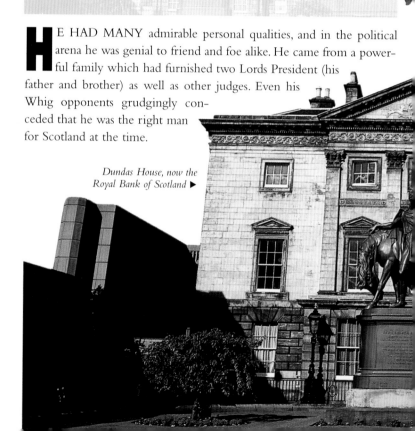

Dundas House, now the Royal Bank of Scotland ▶

Dundas attempted to put right some of the grievous wrongs suffered by the Highlanders at the hands of the Hanoverians. The period of his rule was marked by the dramatic expansion of Scottish trade and industry, the abolition of serfdom, the removal of the proscription on Highland dress (1782) and the restoration in 1784 of the Highland estates forfeited after the Jacobite rebellion.

Fear of French or Spanish invasion in the closing phase of the American War of Independence impelled Dundas to introduce a measure in 1779 enabling magistrates to pressgang seamen for service in the Royal Navy. In 1760 his brother Robert, then Lord Advocate, was reviled for opposing a bill which would have given the Scots their own militia. Not until France again threatened invasion (during the French Revolutionary War) was this measure finally carried, with Dundas himself serving as a private in the Edinburgh Volunteers.

The Friends of the People

THE FRENCH REVOLUTION (1789) was at first greeted sympa-
thetically in Scotland, but as it degenerated into violence, opinion
was sharply divided.

UP TO 1793, when war broke out between France and
Britain, the main support for the ideals of the
Revolution came from the Societies of Friends of the
People, a radical movement that demanded annual parlia-
ments and universal suffrage. A convention of delegates from
these societies took place at Edinburgh in December 1792.
Alarmed at what were seen as seditious activities, Dundas
came down hard on the leaders.

An outspoken Scot, Thomas Muir of Huntershill was
arrested for his support of what he considered the natural
rights of man, and brought to trial in August 1793 before
the notorious Lord Braxfield. Muir was found guilty and
sentenced to 14 years transportation to Botany Bay. The
Rev. Thomas Fyshe Palmer was convicted at Perth a
month later and sentenced to seven years. When a second
convention met in Edinburgh in November 1793 in defiance of the government, three of its leaders, Gerrald,
Margarot and Skirving were likewise sentenced to 14 years
apiece. The severity of these sentences and the rank injustice of the proceedings contrast sharply with similar trials

in England where juries refused to convict Horne Tooke, Thomas Hardy and John Thelwall. In parliament, anti-Scots feeling was stirred up by one John Wilkes, whose ideals were based on his conviction that the English, simply, were a far superior race.

Scotland was in a ferment, and Dundas was frequently burnt in effigy. By 1794, when the Revolution had been replaced by an old-fashioned French war of aggression, the clamour for parliamentary reform gave way to the patriotism of the Volunteers.

▲ *Revolution in France*

The Downfall of Dundas

FROM THE END of the American War in 1783 onwards, Henry Dundas emerged as the political strong man of Scotland. Through a combination of bribery, gerrymandering and pressure he controlled virtually every MP and representative peer in Scotland, delivering to Prime Minister William Pitt, a solid block of Tory supporters.

HIS RULE BECAME increasingly despotic, as his agents and informers permeated Scottish society at all levels, but the government did not reflect the outlook of the people, which was generally Whig. This was represented by the *Edinburgh Review*, which was launched in October 1802 by Sydney Smith, Francis Jeffrey, Lord Brougham and Francis Horner. This magazine attracted a galaxy of talented contributors whose writings on a wide range of topics blew away the cobwebs of Toryism.

The appearance of the *Review* signalled the end of the old regime. In 1805, Dundas, now Viscount Melville and Treasurer of the Navy, was impeached on charges of corruption. He was acquitted the following year and returned briefly to public life before his death in 1811, but his reputation had been tarnished and he never regained his former ascendancy. His place in history has been fiercely debated ever since, though in the context of the times and events through which he lived it must be judged that the benefits he conferred on Scotland outweighed the negative aspects of his rule.

▲ *The tomb of William Pitt, in Westminster Abbey*

The Age of Enlightenment

THE CLOSING DECADES of the eighteenth and the early years of the nineteenth centuries were marked by an extraordinary flowering of the arts and sciences, literature and philosophy that was without parallel anywhere else in the world. Edinburgh became truly the Athens of the North.

SEMINAL WORKS such as David Hume's *Treatise of Human Nature*, Thomas Reid's *Inquiry into the Human Mind*, James Beattie's *Essay on Truth* and Adam Smith's *Wealth of Nations* had a remarkable impact on the civilised world, while the scientific discoveries of Joseph Black, John Leslie, John Gregory, Joseph Hutton, William Cullen and John Hunter in the fields of chemistry, physics, geology, mathematics, anatomy and medicine were quantum leaps in their respective fields and were widely disseminated.

▼ *Edinburgh: 'Athens of the North'*

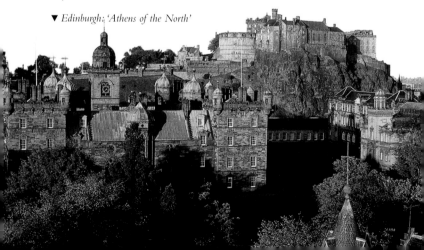

The universities of St Andrews, Glasgow, Aberdeen and Edinburgh, with their 'open door' policies of accepting poor but talented entrants, drew students from England and abroad, while the admirable system of parish schools ensured a steady stream of home-bred undergraduates. Graduates were better-educated than their counterparts in Oxford and Cambridge – Scotland's universities were more in tune with what was required to sustain a growing economy and population. It was at this period that the

▲ *Sir Walter Scott*

tradition of Scottish doctors, engineers, entrepreneurs and colonial administrators was born.

This was also the era of the poet Robert Burns, following in the footsteps of Ramsay and Ferguson, and later of Sir Walter Scott. Along with James Macpherson's *Ossian*, they wielded enormous influence on the development of Romanticism throughout Europe. Although Scotland produced few painters of note, among them may be named Ramsay, Raeburn and Wilkie, all of whom brought new life to portraiture.

The Highland Clearances

THE DESTRUCTION of the clan system, which transformed chiefs into landlords, led eventually to a movement of population that emptied the straths and glens.

THE PROCESS began in the 1760s, when many Highlanders sought a new life in Canada. In light of later developments, it is ironic that this process was initially resisted by Highland landowners, alarmed at the loss of manpower, and consequently a reduction in their rents and prestige. The restoration of the forfeited estates in 1782, and the founda-

▲ *W. B. Hole's depiction of the Clearances*

tion of the (Royal) Highland Society in 1784 did not stem the tide of migration, which accelerated at the beginning of the nineteenth century.

By that time many Highland chiefs had become absentee landlords, living in Edinburgh or London on rents which they raised as often as they could. They were more interested in making their estates pay than the welfare of their clansmen, and so when the demand for wool increased, it became much more lucrative to drive out the people and replace them by Cheviot sheep, large flocks of which could be tended by a single shepherd. Latterly the Clearances were carried out with systematic ruthlessness. In many cases ships were laid on to transport entire communities, to be decanted in Canada. In others, force was used to drive the people out and burn their cottages. Some eked out a precarious existence as fishermen and landless cottars on marginal land, but most emigrated to America, Australia and latterly New Zealand, or flocked to Glasgow, Dundee and other rapidly growing industrial towns. Today, the grassy foundations of farmhouses and even whole villages in many a lonely glen are mute testimony to this shameful episode.

▲ *Many clan chieftains became absentee landlords*

The Industrial Revolution

THE MECHANISATION of industrial production began in Scotland in 1785 with the foundation of New Lanark, harnessing the Clyde to power the textile mills operated by Robert Owen on behalf of his father-in-law, the Glasgow banker and entrepreneur David Dale.

J AMES WATT'S development of an efficient steam engine paved the way for the widespread application of steam power; it was used first in pumping machinery that revolutionised mining, then in a range of stationary engines to operate presses and mills, and finally in the engines that powered locomotives and steamboats. The ready access to coal and iron in the central Lowlands led to the rapid development of heavy engineering, iron foundries, blast furnaces, steel mills and shipbuilding.

Countless other industries developed in their wake, thanks to inventors and entrepreneurs like Charles Tennant (dye-stuffs), Charles Macintosh (rubber-proofing), James Young (paraffin and petroleum), William Collins (publishing) and the Dick brothers (gutta percha).

▲ *Watt's Steam Engine*

There were industrial tramways, with wagons hauled by horses or men, by 1810, but within 20 years steam haulage was becoming commonplace. The turnpike trusts were responsible for the expansion in the road system. The Crinan Canal was built by John Rennie in 1793–1801. John MacAdam is known throughout the world as the father of modern road building; he invented the road surface that helped expand travel and communications, opening up so many areas to so many influences. But the greatest feat of engineering was Thomas Telford's Caledonian Canal through the Great Glen, built in 1804–22 but not completed till 1847. Other canal schemes were soon overtaken by the railways.

▲ *James Watt*

The Radical War, 1819-20

SCOTTISH INDUSTRY boomed during the Napoleonic Wars but slumped in the immediate postwar years. Unemployment of demobilised soldiers was alleviated to some extent by labour used in the building of 'parliamentary' roads and other public projects, but it was also aggravated by the mechanisation of trades which had hitherto been labour-intensive.

HARDEST HIT BY the Industrial Revolution were the handloom weavers, once the aristocrats of labour, whose webs could now be produced as efficiently at a fraction of the cost by mill-hands (mainly young women). As a class, the weavers were well educated and widely read, generally of an independent turn of mind and receptive to radical ideas. A radical conspiracy was uncovered in 1817 and three men were tried for sedition, but one was found not guilty and the other two drew sentences of six months each – a vast difference from the harsh treatment of Muir and Palmer 24 years earlier.

Unrest in England, culminating in the Peterloo Massacre of 1819, led to the passage of the Six Acts prohibiting seditious writings and public meetings. Among the working classes, but mainly the weavers, secret societies plotted revolution. There were riots in Paisley, Greenock and Glasgow, as well as an abortive uprising at Bonnymuir on 5 April 1820, defeated by the Stirlingshire Yeomanry. Of the 47 prisoners arraigned for treason, 24 were sentenced to death, but only three – Wilson, Hardie and Baird – were executed. Of the others, two were found not guilty and the rest were never tried.

▲ *Bismarck and Napoleon – during a time when Scottish industry was booming*

Burgh and Parliamentary Reform

BY 1822, when George IV paid a state visit to Edinburgh (the first made by a reigning sovereign since Charles I), the government of Scotland was dangerously corrupt and unrepresentative. This was hardly a democracy at work; it was easy for London to manipulate the all-too-few voters through appointments, benefits and preferments.

THE LEGACY OF Henry Dundas was that the Lord Advocate was effectively dictator, wielding unlimited power through the distribution of offices and with vast sums of money at his disposal. His son, the second Viscount Melville, 'managed' Scotland in the Tory interest from 1811 till 1827, and, so long as he was in power, political reform was doomed to failure.

The representation of Scotland was still as it was fixed by the Act of Union in 1707. Some towns, which returned a

▲ Edinburgh, visited by George IV in 1822

member to parliament, had dwindled in importance, whereas others (notably Greenock) were wholly unrepresented. The electorate in the country districts was so small that in 1822, when the population of Scotland stood at 2,100,000, the county voters numbered fewer than 3,000. The situation in the burghs was even worse. The town councils were self-elected and only they had the power to choose their MP.

The return of the Whigs to power paved the way, at last, for parliamentary and burgh reform. By the Reform Act of 1832, the new population centres were given representation in Parliament. The number of

voting electors in Edinburgh went up from 39 to over 9,000, and the number of Scottish MPs was increased to 53. In Robert Wallace, Greenock got a member who played a prominent part in the introduction of Uniform Penny Postage in 1840, among other reforms. The franchise was extended in the counties to holders of land worth £10 a year as well as some tenants, while residents of the burghs were given the vote if they occupied houses valued at £10 a year.

▲ *Presentation of the Act of Union in 1707*

Chartism in Scotland

THE REFORM ACT broke the back of Toryism in Scotland. In the parliament elected in 1833, 41 Scottish MPs were Whigs and only 12 Tories. One of its first acts was to abolish the corrupt burgh corporations and restore the rights of citizens to elect town councils.

SWEEPING AS THESE reforms were, they did not go far enough. Euphoria rapidly gave way to discontent and a growing sense of grievance among the working classes who remained without the vote. Unemployment remained high and was exacerbated by the steady influx not only of Highlanders but also Irish who were settling in the south-west of Scotland even before the Hungry Forties. A commission of enquiry into the conditions of the poor (1843–44) led to a Poor Law Amendment Act for Scotland in 1845, setting a legal poor rate and extending the system of workhouses.

▲ *A parish workhouse*

Against this background of rising poverty developed the Chartist movement, which took its name from the People's Charter, with its six points: adult male suffrage, secret ballots, equal electoral districts, salaried MPs, the abolition of property qualifications and annual parliaments. Some of these aims had been advocated by the Friends of the People. As earlier attempts to form unions had failed, much of the workers' energy was thus channelled into the Chartists, who sincerely believed that they could bring about a democratic parliament and an enfranchised working class to redress their grievances. The Chartist movement peaked in 1847 but lost some credibility when it was found that many of the signatures on its lengthy petition to parliament were false. Though it died down by 1849 all of its recommendations (except annual elections) were later incorporated in the Reform Acts of 1867–68, 1884–85 and later.

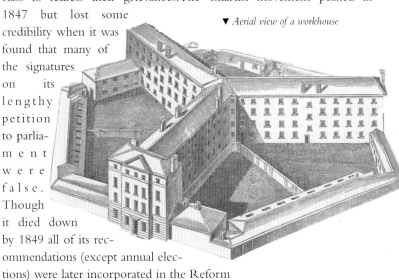

▼ *Aerial view of a workhouse*

The Great Disruption, 1843

THE CHURCH OF SCOTLAND, established at the Revolution, underwent a number of changes over the ensuing 150 years, reflecting the outlook and attitudes of the times.

BECAUSE OF ITS democratic constitution it was prone to argument between moderates and extremists which often resulted in schism. Apart from the Cameronians who remained aloof after the Revolution, there were the followers of Ebenezer Erskine who were expelled in 1740 and formed the First Secession Church or Seceders. In 1746, some of the Seceders baulked at the Burgher's Oath (an admission of 'true religion') and broke away to form anti-burgher congregations, a breach that was not mended till 1820.

In the late eighteenth century argument raged between the Auld Lichts and New Lichts, as the conservative and radical wings of the Church were popular-ly known. More serious was

the vexed question of patronage; many 'intruded' ministers, foisted on congregations by the local laird, were subjected to verbal and physical abuse, and riots at their ordination, were only prevented by a strong military presence.

This uneasy situation continued for many years, until the General Assembly of 1841, by a large majority, passed a resolution calling for the end of lay patronage. When this was ignored by the government, the Non-Intrusionists resolved in November 1842 to secede from the Church if this injustice was not put right. At the General Assembly on 18 May 1843, 400 ministers withdrew and established the Free Church of Scotland, with Dr Thomas Chalmers as Moderator.

▼ *Edinburgh's Assembly Hall, where the General Assemblies of 1841 and 1843 were held*

Religious Division

TWO-FIFTHS OF THE CLERGY and congregations of the Church of Scotland broke away in 1843. They had to vacate their parish churches but lost no time in erecting churches of their own. Hostile landlords often refused them a site, but from the outset the Free Church was well-organised, with ample funds and its own theological college.

IRONICALLY, PATRONAGE, which was the main bone of contention in 1843, did not survive the Disruption, though it was not formally abolished till 1874. Its abolition did not heal the breach between the two churches, which had grown apart in the interim. Such matters as education and poor relief, hitherto the responsibility of the Church, were surrendered to purely secular bodies, the parish school boards and the Inspectors of the Poor.

Doctrinally, there was no difference between the churches, but a further split occurred in 1892 when the conservative wing of the Free Church seceded in 1892 to form the Free Presbyterian Church, whose congregations were mainly in the west Highlands and Islands. Meanwhile, the United Presbyterians were formed from the bulk of earlier secessionist bodies, and in 1900 they joined forces with the Free Church to form the United Free Church. Inevitably some congregations remained aloof from this union and continued as the Free Church ('the wee Frees'). Similarly, in 1929, when the United Free Church rejoined the Church of Scotland, a few congregations retained their independence as the United Free Church Continuing.

John Calvin, the root of Scottish religious reform ▶

The Development of Heavy Engineering, 1840-1900

THE HEYDAY OF Scottish heavy engineering was the second half of the nineteenth century. During that period, output in every field of industry rose astronomically and peaked about 1890. Although production began to decline after that date, due largely to competition from Germany and the USA, it was still a major force till the end of the First World War.

THE MINING OF coal peaked in the 1890s, when Lanarkshire's coalfields alone yielded 17 million tonnes per annum and the mines of Ayrshire and Dunbartonshire produced a further 5 million tonnes.

Blackband ironstone, the basis of the region's iron and steel industry, rose steadily from 1840 till 1880 when it reached a record level of 2.2 million tonnes per annum, but within a decade this had fallen to about a third and continued to fall by 100,000 tonnes a decade until the 1920s, by which time output was negligible.

▲ *Mining museum at Wanlockhead*

In 1788 the total steel output of Scottish blast furnaces was about 6,000 tonnes. Between 1823 and 1843 this rose from 31,000 to 250,000 tonnes and it continued to grow until 1900 when it reached its peak of 1,200,000 tonnes, more than a third of the total British production. In 1885, there were 125 blast furnaces in the west of Scotland alone, together with numerous mills for the manufacture of steel plate, wire and ingots. Thereafter, an increasing amount of pig iron had to be imported in order to keep pace with demand, as the native ores became exhausted. Iron foundries produced all manner of finished goods, from bath-taps to gigantic watervalves. Prefabricated iron bridges were exported all over the world, from Tower Bridge, London to the Elizabeth Bridge in Budapest. One of the most famous iron works was the Carron Ironworks, whose light cannon, or 'carronades' became a standard weapon of armies all over the world.

Scotland's most famous iron structure –
the Forth Rail Bridge ▶

Shipbuilding

IT WAS IN THE field of shipbuilding that Scotland led the world in the nineteenth century. Patrick Miller of Dalswinton's steamboat of 1788 was followed by the *Charlotte Dundas* (1802) and Henry Bell's *Comet* (1812), the first practical, passenger-carrying steamboat on the Clyde. In 1818 the *Margery*, built by William Denny at Dumbarton, was the first steamboat to cross the Channel.

BY 1823, SCOTLAND had built 95 steamships. Even before the general adaptation of the steam engine to marine engineering, however, the dredging of the Clyde had allowed Glasgow to accept ocean-going vessels and to rise quickly as Scotland's leading port. David Napier was the first to adapt steampower for deep-sea vessels; by mid-century he was one of the world's foremost mechanical engineers. Napier and

▲ Steamboat on the Clyde *by William Danniell*

his cousin Robert, along with Tod & Macgregor of Partick, pioneered iron ships. Ocean-going paddle-steamers, built for Samuel Cunard, were crossing the Atlantic by 1838. Screw propulsion soon followed and by 1860 Clyde-built ships were to be found on every sea, lake and navigable river in the world.

The American Civil War was a boom time, as the Clyde built faster and faster steamers for the Confederates to beat the Union blockade. In 1901, Robert MacIntyre boasted that the Clyde had produced more first-class ships than all the other shipbuilding rivers of the world put together. In addition to merchant ships, the Clyde yards turned out battleships and cruisers for the world's navies. Most of the capital ships in the Russo-Japanese War – on both sides – were Clyde-built.

In the twentieth century, John Brown built the *Queen Mary* and the *Queen Elizabeth*, then the largest ships afloat, but their successor the *Queen Elizabeth II* (1969) was the swan song of the industry.

◀ *The* Queen Mary

Tourism

THOMAS PENNANT and Samuel Johnson paid visits to Scotland in the late eighteenth century and their impressions of the country were later published. William and Dorothy Wordworth went in search of Burns Country in 1803, while the novels of Sir Walter Scott brought Mendelssohn to Scotland in 1829. But it was none other than Queen Victoria herself who set the fashion for Highland holidays, and thus set the tourist industry in motion.

Queen Victoria, painted in 1887

QUEEN VICTORIA, accompanied by Prince Albert, paid her first visit to Scotland in 1842, the first reigning monarch since George IV in 1822. It was Queen Victoria who was so anxious to make amends to the Scots for the harm done to them in former years; Albert even took to wearing a kilt on trips to the Highlands, and spoke highly of the inhabitants. The country made such a favourable impression on Victoria that when she departed on 15 September she vowed to return. More extensive tours followed in 1844 and 1847.

When the Queen visited Deeside in 1848 it was love at first sight. Through the good offices of the prime minister, Lord Aberdeen, the Queen obtained the lease of the Balmoral estate, which was purchased outright in 1852 along with Birkhall and part of neighbouring estates. Balmoral Castle was completed in 1855, and from then until her death in 1901 (and especially after the death of Prince Albert in 1861) Victoria spent more and more of her time there. The Queen's example was dutifully followed by the nobilitiy who came north for the grouse shooting, and the fashion for Scotland and things Scottish (including kilts and tartan) spread southwards.

At the same time, better rail and steamer communications, as well as paid holidays, brought English tourists of all classes to Scotland, a tradition that continued unabated until the era of cheap foreign travel in the 1960s.

▲ *Balmoral Castle*

The Crofters' Commission, 1886

ALTHOUGH tourism has now become the mainstay of the Highlands and Islands, it initially had adverse effects. The fashion for grouse-shooting, deerstalking and salmon fishing brought sporting tenants but did nothing to alleviate the misery and destitution of the crofters and cottars.

ALTHOUGH ENFORCED clearances were, by 1880, a thing of the past, voluntary emigration had continued unabated. Uncontrolled grazing by sheep destroyed soil fertility, and many of the sheep farms were turned into deer forests for the sporting gentry. There were no longer enough opportunities for everyone to remain or become a fisherman or crofter. To the landless cottars and crofters whose holdings had

been sub divided to the point at which they were scarcely viable, such development understandably caused bitter resentment.

Unrest in the Highlands over rent increases was exacerbated in 1882 by the arbitrary actions of estate factors, the immediate cause of trouble being the withdrawal of pasturage rights from the crofters of The Braes in Skye. A Highland Land League (organised on the same lines as the Irish Land League)

▲ *All crofters benefitted from the Highland Land League*

agitated for reform, and rioting was curbed by sending troops and gun-
boats to the affected districts.

A royal commission under Lord Napier was appointed to enquire
into crofters' grievances. This resulted in the Crofters' Holdings Act
(1886), which established the Crofters' Commission and guaranteed
fixity of tenure, fair rents and compensation for land improvements. The
Congested Districts Boards of the 1890s and the Highlands and Islands
Development Board in more recent times have done much to alleviate the
problems of these remote areas.

▲ *Crofters on Skye*

Emigration and Immigration

IN 1755, the Reverend Alexander Webster compiled the first census of the Scottish population from returns submitted by parish ministers. By this means it was estimated that the population numbered 1,265,380. At the first government census (1801) it had risen to 1,608,420.

THE DECENNIAL census conducted from 1841 onwards showed a steady increase in population overall, but the figures for the counties in the Highlands and Islands showed a notable decrease in each decade, reflecting the effect of the Clearances and later economic deprivation. By 1901, the population had risen to almost 4.5 million and it peaked at around 5 million in 1921. At the 1931 census, the last to be taken before the Second World War, the population had decreased by 0.8% to 4,842,980. Since then the population has remained fairly static.

This reflects badly when compared with statistics for England and Wales. In 1700 the English population was five times that of Scotland, but by 1801 it was six times greater and since 1901 it has been almost nine times greater. As the birthrate in both countries has been much the same, the reason

A family of 12 leaving for Canada ▶

for Scotland's relative decline has been emigration, mainly to the USA, Canada, Australia and New Zealand.

Between 1832 and 1870 there was a substantial influx of Irish, forced to flee their native land as a result of the potato famine, to the industrial districts, particularly Lanarkshire; though it declined thereafter it has remained a significant factor. Jews from Russia and later Central Europe, Italians and Poles were the largest immigrant groups from 1900 onwards.

Changes in Local and Central Government

ALTHOUGH SCOTLAND could boast a higher standard of literacy than England, as well as a strong radical tradition, it remained relatively under represented in parliament, and suffered political neglect as a result.

THIS ANOMALY was gradually put right, beginning with the Reform Act of 1884 which replaced the old burgh and county constituencies by new ones based on population. The following year the Scottish Office in London was created, but 40 years would elapse before

its head attained cabinet rank as a Secretary of State and was relocated in St Andrews House, Edinburgh. In 1888, Lord Goschen devised a formula which entitled Scotland to a share of government money in the ratio of 11 parts to England's 80, to reflect Scotland's contribution in taxes to the national exchequer.

Local government was drastically overhauled from 1889 onwards by the creation of county councils. Boards of Education and Supervision of the Poor Law did much to standardise teaching and the care of the elderly and infirm, and by the Education Act of 1872 free education became compulsory for children between the ages of five and 13 (as well as helping the population to become more literate, this furthered the decline of the Celtic languages, though this was of little concern to the government). A Scottish Public Health Act was passed in 1867, though by that time Glasgow and other major cities had already taken their own initiative to improve sanitation and provide a clean water supply. Nevertheless, poverty and destitution remained a major problem, while the run down inner areas of the cities had degenerated into some of the worst slums in Europe.

◀ *Edinburgh, where the Scottish Office was eventually relocated*

The Birth of Socialism, 1890-1914

SCOTTISH NATIONALISM of a negative character, fuelled by resentment of the injustice and inequity (real or imagined) of Westminster rule, gave way in the late 1880s to socialism.

T HE REFORM ACT OF 1884 had extended the franchise to many working men. Paradoxically the Liberals, who had done so much to bring this about, now went into a period of decline. Keir Hardie (grandson of the martyr of 1820) led the radical movement which resulted in the foundation of the Scottish Labour Party in 1888 and the Independent Labour Party (ILP) in 1893. As the fortunes of the Liberal party declined the working classes looked to socialism, and in 1892 Hardie became the first workingman to enter the Commons as Independent Labour member for South West Ham. From there, things progressed. In 1900, when the Labour Representative Committee (LRC) was formed, he became MP for Merthyr, Wales. Although, as a

Keir Hardie statue, Cumnock ▶

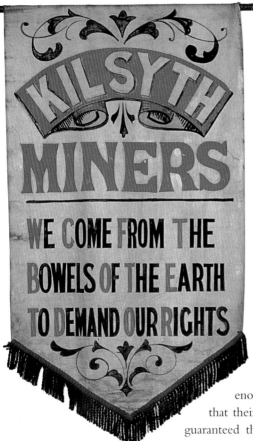

socialist, Hardie represented English or Welsh constituencies, he was also an ardent nationalist, campaigning for Home Rule in Scotland and Ireland.

The ILP was affiliated to the LRC, which became the Labour Party in 1906. Salaries for MPs, advocated by the Chartists in the 1840s, were introduced in 1911, making working class representation more feasible. In the same period, trade unionism, especially among the miners and factory workers, made enormous strides; they saw that their rights would only be guaranteed through legislation. The Co-operative movement developed rapidly between 1880 and 1914.

▲ *Many miners joined trade unions*

Edwardian Scotland

THE EDWARDIAN ERA (1901–10) is often regarded as a halcyon age: at one end of the time scale, the celebrations that marked the return of troops from the Boer War; at the other, the great Lanark Aviation Meeting of 1910 which showed that Scotland was in the forefront of the latest technology.

THE PERIOD WAS encapsulated by the two great exhibitions held in Glasgow, in 1901 and 1911, at which the achievements of the Second City of the Empire were paraded before the world. It was a time seemingly of long, hot summers, of trips 'doon the watter', when seaside resorts from Largs and Troon in the west to Arbroath in the east thronged with carefree holidaymakers. Perhaps this image of the Edwardian era has been created by the picture postcard craze, for the reality was very different.

The stark fact is that Scotland in the early years of the twentieth century lagged far behind England and the other developed countries in such

Edward VII ▶

matters as housing, health, life expectancy and infant mortality. Maternal mortality, despite the pioneering work of Joseph Lister at Glasgow in anti-sepsis, was actually higher in 1910 than it had been in 1870. A high proportion of the urban population lived in 'single-ends', one-room apartments. In such gross overcrowding tuberculosis was rife. Sanitary arrangements, even the elementary earth closet, were often non-existent and wells were polluted by raw sewage. Levels of overcrowding in the city slums, uncontrolled industrial toxic waste and diseases of malnutrition like rickets were unacceptably high.

▲ *Design in the Edwardian era: Charles Rennie Mackintosh*

The First World War, 1914–18

KEIR HARDIE strove, through the *Socialist International*, to call a general strike of the working classes in Europe in the event of war. The complete failure of this organisation at this crucial time broke Hardie, who died in 1915.

WHEN WAR BROKE out in August 1914, it was time to put aside major industrial grievances. Joined by a common cause against the enemy, Scots responded enthusiastically to the call to arms. Many were Royal Navy reservists, mobilised within days, but followed shortly by

the Scottish regiments. The Glasgow Highlanders and fifth Scottish Rifles were the first Territorial battalions to join the British Expeditionary Force. Before the war's end the Highland Light Infantry had raised over 30 battalions, making it the largest infantry regiment in the army.

▲ *Scottish troops on the Western Front*

Scots fought in every campaign and in every branch of the services. Almost 75,000 were killed in action. A higher proportion of gallantry medals went to Scots than the rest of the United Kingdom, no fewer than 13 Glasgow men winning the Victoria Cross. The long lists of names on the war memorials to be found in every town and village testify to the disproportionate sacrifice of Scotland in that conflict. Scottish nurses played a prominent part in Flanders and the Balkans.

On the home front, factories went over to war production, employing mainly women for the duration of the war. Though less affluent than England, Scotland raised more per capita for the 1917 War Loan, Glasgow alone raising £14,171,760 including £5.25 million in a single day, more than twice the total for Birmingham.

▲ Scottish Soldiers Return *by François Flameng*

Red Clydeside

SINCE THE RADICAL WAR of 1820, Glasgow had a reputation for left-wing political views. It had been a stronghold of militant Chartism in the 1840s and was in the forefront of socialist development from the 1880s onwards.

A GLASGOW schoolmaster, John Maclean, was the leading propagandist for socialism. In the 20 years between joining the Social Democratic Federation (1903) and his early death (1923), Maclean was the outstanding figure in Scottish socialism. Indeed, his international status was such that Lenin ranked him with Karl Liebknecht in Germany and Friedrich Adler in Austria; in January 1918 he was appointed first Bolshevik Consul for Britain.

Maclean eventually rejected Communism and worked to establish a Scottish Workers' Republic. Strongly influenced by James Connolly (the Edinburgh man who became the Irish workers' leader and was executed for his part in the Easter Rising, 1916), Maclean was also an ardent supporter of Irish nationalism.

When landlords raised rents, tenants went on rent strikes which were eventually settled by the Rent Restriction Act (1915). Clashes between workers and management in the shipyards and armaments factories over rates of pay and working conditions led to strikes which were brutally suppressed, shop stewards and 'agitators' like Maclean being sent to prison. The worst incident took place on 31 January 1919 when strikers clashed with police in George Square, Glasgow. Armed troops and

Shipbuilding in Clydeside ▶

tanks moved in the following day. By contrast, industrial action between 1919 and 1939 was comparatively slight, owing to better union-management negotiating structures.

Postwar Depression

SCOTLAND was not the land fit for heroes which politicians had promised when the war was over. With so much loss of life, many questioned just what Scotland's role would be in the preservation of an empire tthat they had helped build. In parts of the Highlands and Islands, returned servicemen took the law into their own hands and raided the large estates to carve out crofts for themselves.

THE WARTIME boom in shipbuilding and heavy engineering had disguised the harsh economic reality that Scotland's steelworks lagged behind those of Germany and the USA, or that her coal was of relatively poor quality and cost more to extract. The sharp downturn in world trade from 1919 onwards hit Scotland harder than the rest of the United Kingdom. Unemploy-ment rose well above the national average, and few of the newer industries were located in Scotland by way of compensation for the decline in the traditional forms of employment.

Dissatisfaction with the government's inability or reluctance to address these problems found expression in political trends, with a resurgence of nationalism as well as a decided move to the left. The compromise between these forces was the continuation of the Independent Labour Party in Scotland, which, instead of joining with mainstream Labour and exerting a direct influence on its policies, stood aloof. At the general election of 1922, 10 ILP members were elected to parliament

from constituencies in the west of Scotland, perpetuating the myth of Red Clydeside and deterring the newer industries from establishing factories there.

▲ *Traditional employments, such as mining, declined*

The Rise of Scottish Nationalism

ALTHOUGH seldom finding political expression, there had been a strong undercurrent of nationalism in Scotland ever since the union of 1707. Scottish MPs, whatever their party, always formed an identifiable group, reflected in their voting pattern whenever Scottish interests were affected.

BETWEEN 1885 AND 1895, a Crofters' party, created at the time of Highland unrest, held five seats in each of the three parliaments of that decade, but apart from specific matters pertaining to crofting they voted solidly with the Liberals. By contrast, both Conservative and Labour parties in the period after the First World War, while representing the Scottish electorate in a British context, also operated within Scottish organisations at grass-roots level, and often co-operated with each other in matters of Scottish interest.

By 1894, the Liberals were committed to Home Rule for both Scotland and Ireland, and the Scottish Home Rule Bill passed its second reading by a large majority in 1913. The war shelved this proposal and in the immediate postwar climate it found little enthusiasm. Attempts to revive a Home Rule bill failed in 1924 and 1926.

A specifically Scottish national party began to develop as the ILP went into decline, but went hand in hand with a resurgence of Scottish culture and renewed interest in Gaelic and the vernacular of Lowland Scotland. The National Party of Scotland was founded in April 1928 and became the Scottish National Party in 1934, but although it fielded candidates in many constituencies it did not succeed in capturing any seats, the result of many years of internal squabbles. It was not until after 1945 that the organisation would make any effective political progress.

▲ *Liberals wanted Home Rule for both Scotland and Ireland*

The Local Government Act, 1929

AT THE BEGINNING of the twentieth century Scotland was governed at a local level by 33 county councils, 200 burgh councils, 869 parish councils and nearly 1,000 parish school boards. Such proliferation produced considerable overlap in functions and responsibilities, and became increasingly unwieldy.

I N ENGLAND AND WALES the operation of locally elected bodies was considerably streamlined, largely as a result of the Education Act of 1902. A comparable Act for Scotland was not passed till 1918, replacing the parish school boards by education authorities in the counties and five largest cities. Other areas of local government were not altered until the passage of the Local Government (Scotland) Act in 1929.

▲ *Assembly Hall, Edinburgh today*

Apart from the burgh and county councils, all other local authorities were abolished. Glasgow, Edinburgh, Aberdeen and Dundee became counties of cities, the existing county councils were reorganised, Perth and Kinross and Moray and Nairn were combined for most functions, 20 large burghs (with at least 20,000 inhabitants) were given full powers except in education and valuation, 171 small burghs had minor powers confined to housing, sanitation, streets, public house licensing, parks and amenities, and 199 district councils replaced the parish councils. Over the ensuing years other bodies were created for specific functions: 11 fire areas, 13 water boards and 20 police authorities, as well as boards dealing with cemeteries and the probation service.

▲ *Perth today: combined by Act with Kinross*

Special Areas

THE INDEPENDENCE of Scottish industry and commerce was severely eroded by the First World War. The five Scottish railways merged
in 1923 to become part of the LMS or LNER. Many Scottish firms
were taken over by English companies and suffered as a result. Even
the Scottish banks, while retaining their distinctive notes, were
often under English control.

AS THE POSTWAR depression deepened, Scotland suffered dispro-
portionately badly. Scottish branches or subsidiaries of British companies were often the first to close down; and while England began to
recover in the mid-1930s, Scotland was still feeling the effects of the depression until the approach of war in 1938 gave fresh impetus to heavy industry,
when all in Britain were pulled together yet again in the face of an enemy.

This depression resulted in a severe problem of unemployment and
widespread destitution with which the ordinary relief measures could not
cope. Nevertheless, it was not until 1934 that the Special Areas (Development
and Improvement) Act was passed. A commissioner for the special areas in
Scotland was empowered to give men temporary work on projects of public improvement, as well as create land settlement schemes. Additional powers were given in 1937, which led to the creation of trading and industrial
estates to attract new enterprises to underprivileged areas, the first being
established at Hillington, Renfrewshire, on the south-western outskirts of
Glasgow, in 1937–38. Most of this development was financed by the government, but it included a trust fund of £2 million set up by Lord Nuffield.

Economic crisis struck postwar Scotland ▶

The Royal Bank of Scotland plc
ONE POUND
STERLING
£1
AGB0950000
AGB1100000
ALEXANDER GRAHAM BELL 1847–1922
The Royal Bank of Scotland plc

The Second World War

ECONOMIC RECOVERY did not come to Scotland until the rearmament programme got under way in 1938. The war led to the creation of many new factories and the expansion of existing plants. The exigencies of war also produced short-term improvements, especially in parts of the Highlands and Islands where naval, military and air bases were established.

MANY OF THE WARTIME airfields, from Machrihanish and Crossapol (Tiree) to Balivanich (Benbecula) and Sumburgh (Shetland), would eventually produce lasting benefits in the post-war era, but the great naval base at Scapa Flow, developed during the First World War, was soon almost as obsolete as the great battleships it was created to protect. However the naval dockyard at Rosyth and the submarine base on the Clyde got a new lease of life in the Cold War period.

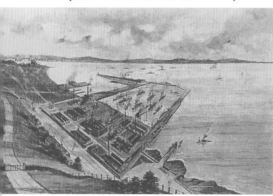

Many thousands of Scots were conscripted into the armed forces, and acquitted themselves as well as their fathers had done in 1914, but the civil population was also affected.

▲ *Naval dockyard at Rosyth*

The only major air raids, aimed at Clyde shipping, destroyed Clydebank but Scotland never received the heavy bombing that was the incentive to tackle the chronic problem of the slums in London.

The main benefit to arise from the war was a renewal of national spirit and a feeling that, having survived the conflict, there was a will to deal resolutely with social problems. This was reflected in the general election of 1945, in which 40 seats went to Labour, compared with 25 to the Conservatives, five to the Liberals and four to minor parties. Scottish Nationalist Robert MacIntyre was elected to parliament, a clear sign of the new spirit, even though he was defeated shortly afterwards in the general election. Two years later, a daring raid was made on Westminster Abbey, to take back the Stone of Scone.

▼ *A piper moves ashore during the D-Day landings*

The New Towns

WITH ALMOST 40% of the population of Scotland concentrated in the Glasgow area, much of it housed in grossly overcrowded slums, a radical solution to the housing problem was sought. Vast housing schemes on the outskirts of the city, at Drumchapel, Easterhouse and other suburbs, coped with an overspill of 200,000.

A MORE RADICAL answer was Patrick Abercrombie's Clyde Valley Regional Plan (1945), which envisaged a reduction in the population of Glasgow from about 1,000,000 to 600,000, the overspill to be located in four satellite towns built from scratch. For political reasons this proposal was strenuously opposed by Glasgow's Labour-dominated

corporation, which feared that relocation would weaken its position. For the same reason, the New Town concept was taken up enthusiastically by the Conservatives from 1951 onwards.

The New Towns were to be funded, planned and controlled by their own development corporations, appointed by the Secretary

▲ *Cumbernauld New Town*

of State for Scotland and financed by the government from taxes, rather than rates raised locally.

The first of the new towns was East Kilbride, work on which commenced in 1948. Cumbernauld (Stirlingshire), Livingston (West Lothian) and Irvine (Ayrshire) were eventually established, though not without the continuing opposition of local authorities. Plans for a fifth New Town, at Stonehouse in Lanarkshire, were aborted in 1974. Elsewhere, Glenrothes (1949) was originally planned as a new town for the Fife coalfield, but was rapidly transformed into a major centre of light industry.

As well as dealing with the problem of slums, this new social infrastructure was an attempt to compensate for losses in the heavy industries and to attract new industries north of the border, thereby creating a healthy domestic economy.

▲ *Many new homes were built*

The Scottish Economy

PLANNING OF SCOTLAND'S postwar economy may be said to have begun as early as 1941 under Tom Johnston. During the period of the Attleegovernment, Johnston, as Secretary of State for Scotland, boasted justifiably that he achieved more for his country as a British cabinet minister than he would if Scotland had its own parliament in Edinburgh.

THE SCOTTISH economy certainly benefited materially under a Labour administration. While a strong figure like Johnston ensured that postwar reforms were given a Scottish dimension, nationalisation of traditional industries like coalmining and the ramifications of the Welfare State (notably the National Health Service) gave the Scots every incentive for maintaining the political status quo. When Labour returned to power in 1964 the mantle of Tom Johnston fell on Willie Ross, in whose forceful hands the Scottish Office achieved an unprecedented measure of independence from London.

During the period of Conservative rule (1951–64), a swing against the government at the 1959 election led to an enquiry into the Scottish economy, whose report was published in 1961. This recommended regional planning and development, implemented in June 1962 by the establishment of the Scottish Development Department, shortly followed by the Scottish Home and Health Department. A Scottish Economic Plan was unveiled in 1966 and led to the Scottish Economic Planning Department (1973), which assumed responsibility for power, transport and oil support services, as well as general economic planning.

Oil Rig, Firth of Tay ▶

Local Government Act, 1973

THE LOCAL GOVERNMENT (Scotland) Act of 1973 was the outcome of a Royal Commission, chaired by Lord Wheatley, who delivered his report in 1969 and summarised the shortcomings of the existing system as 'complications, illogicalities, expense and ineffectiveness'. The 1973 Act came into effect in May 1975 and was the most radical shake-up since 1929.

BY 1973 THERE were 21 large burghs, 176 small burghs and the same number of city, county and district councils as before. Wheatley recommended that the burgh councils be scrapped and the entire system replaced by a two-tier administration of nine mainland regions and three island authorities on the first level, and 53 districts on the second level.

The regions would be responsible for strategic planning, transport, roads, water, sewerage, education, registration, social work and police. The authorities in the Western Isles, Orkney and Shetland had similar responsibilities, but shared with Highland Region in police, fire and social services, as well as some aspects of education. The districts were responsible for local planning, urban and rural development, housing, environment, parks, recreation and libraries.

The map of Scotland was redrawn and immediately attracted fierce criticism. Highland Region occupied a third of the total land area but had a population of only 180,000. Strathclyde, occupying a sixth of the area, had 2,466,300 inhabitants, half the population of Scotland. These regions proved to be too unwieldy to give any sense of local democracy.

A map showing Local Government Reorganisation, 1975 ▶

REGIONAL AND ISLAND
AUTHORITIES

SHETLAND

Fair Isle

ORKNEY

WESTERN
ISLES

St. Kilda

Inverness

Skye

HIGHLAND

GRAMPIAN

Aberdeen

TAYSIDE

Mull

Dundee

CENTRAL

FIFE

Glasgow

Edinburgh

LOTHIAN

Islay

STRATHCLYDE

BORDERS

DUMFRIES &
GALLOWAY

Resurgence of Nationalism

IN APRIL 1945, Robert McIntyre won Motherwell for the Scottish National Party (SNP) in a by-election. The seat reverted to Labour at the general election a few weeks later and it was not until 1970 that Scottish National Party again won a by-election, when Winifred Ewing took Hamilton.

FRUSTRATED AT THE BALLOT BOX, the nationalists sought other means of raising public awareness, through Scottish National Assemblies which publicly debated major issues, and through the traditional method of a Scottish Covenant, a mammoth petition organised in October 1949. Only in the 1960s, as Britain declined as a world power, did Scottish nationalism make real headway.

Victory at Hamilton in 1970 proved to be no freak result. At the general election of February 1974 the SNP won seven seats and increased this to 11 at the election the following October. This upsurge coincided with the discovery of North Sea oil, giving Scots a new sense of their importance as a nation

The face of Scottish Nationalism ▶

and helping allay the old fears of so many that Scotland could not exist apart from England in economic terms. Devolution dominated British politics in the late 1970s and led to the Scotland Act (1978) which entailed a referendum for a Scottish assembly in March 1979. On a relatively low turnout, 51.6 per cent voted yes but fell below the 40 per cent of the electorate required. The measure failed because it was associated with a declining Britain in general and the poor performance of the Labour government in particular. Far from being the solution to Scotland's desire for home rule, it was regarded as an inadequate alternative to a continuation of the union.

▲ *Traditional Scottish dress is still very important today*

The Thatcher Years and Beyond

IMPATIENCE, exasperation and insensitivity to the aspirations of the Scots were the keynotes of the Thatcher administration (1979–90), and go far to explain the sharp decline in Scottish Conservative support during this period.

THOUGH PERSONALLY POPULAR in Scotland, her successor John Major proved ineffectual in reversing the Tory decline. At the 1992 general election, despite a slight increase in Tory support, the party performed poorly, holding on to only 11 out of 72 seats; but this was as nothing compared with the total eclipse in 1997, when the Conservatives were left without a single seat north of the border.

At the same time, having been one of the least enthusiastic parts of the United Kingdom with regard to the European Community in the early 1970s, Scotland gradually changed tack in the 1980s and became strongly pro-European. The SNP articulated this sea-change in its policy of 1988, which embraced the doctrine of subsidiarity, whereby small nations

▲ *Prime Minister Margaret Thatcher was unpopular in Scotland* could preserve an independent identity within the larger framework of a united Europe.

One of the last acts of John Major's government was the repatriation of the Stone of Destiny in 1996, exactly 700 years after it was seized by Edward I and removed to Westminster. It was not restored to its traditional resting place at Scone but placed for safe-keeping in Edinburgh Castle. Its return symbolised the new-found confidence and self-assertiveness of the Scots, in whom the spirit of nationhood was now stronger than at any time since before 1707: Scotland is still very much a Celtic nation, however much its identity has been watered down over the centuries.

◀ *Repatriation of the Stone of Destiny*

Whither Devolution?

INCREASINGLY SINCE 1992, politics in Scotland have resolved into a straight contest between Labour and the SNP. Recognising the aspiration of the Scots to a greater say in their own government, Labour proposed a system of devolution. On coming to power in 1997, Tony Blair honoured this promise, which led to the referendum on Scotland's future.

THE ELECTORATE were given the choice of saying yes or no to two questions: should Scotland have its own parliament, and should such a body be given tax-varying powers? The result was overwhelmingly in favour of the first, but even the controversial second question received a clear affirmative.

Ever since the referendum of 1979, the prospect of a Scottish parliament seemed inevitable, and steps were taken to prepare a suitable venue. The Parliament House in the High Street of Edinburgh (now the seat of the Scottish legal establishment) being unsuitable, an alternative was found in the shape of Edinburgh's Royal High School, which was extensively modernised in the 1980s. But as the prospect of an actual parliament draws nearer a fresh site in Edinburgh's Old Town is now being developed. From 1999, Scotland will have a reduced representation at Westminster, which will continue to control defence and foreign affairs. It remains to be seen whether the Scots will be content with a measure of autonomy or, as the SNP urges, use devolution as a stepping-stone to full independence.

Scots in general are approaching the Millennium with cautious optimism.

▲ *Alex Salmond, SNP leader*

Tony Blair supports Devolution ▶▶

Glossary

BASQUES

These people inhabit an area of northern Spain and south-west France. They have their own language and culture and struggle for independence from Spain and France.

BRONZE AGE

The use of bronze became wide-spread in Scotland in about 2000 BC. The metal probably arrived from Ireland and dominated met-allurgy until about 400 BC.

BURIAL MOUNDS

As part of the Neolithic peoples' burial customs they often interred their dead, with grave goods, under raised heaps of earth and stone.

CAIRNS

Common in Scotland, cairns were used to mark a specific site by heaping local stones into a mound. Sometimes used to mark graves, or built as a memorial.

COVENANTERS

These extreme Presbyterians raised armies against King Charles in the seventeenth century in order to defend their doctrine of extreme absolutism.

CROUCHED CORPSES

The Beaker peoples, who flourished from 2500–1500 BC, often interred their corpses in this position as part of their burial customs.

DEVOLUTION

where a country, or state, breaks away from its governing country and forms an independent parlia-ment. It became a real possibility during the 1970s with the rise of the Scottish National Party (SNP).

FEUDAL OVERLORD

The overlord was loyal to the crown and controlled land which the peasants worked for him.

THE FEUDAL SYSTEM

This Anglo-Norman system arose from the dual need for military protection and food production. It was a system by which lords protected their tenants in return for services, such as loyalty in battle. The Earl ofNorthumberland introduced it to Scotland in the 1100s.

HANOVERIANS

The Hanovarians were supporters of the British monarchs from the House of Hanover (1692–1815) in Germany. The line was introduced with the reign of George I.

HIGHLANDS

This area of north-west Scotland has traditionally remained Celtic- and Gaelic-speaking while the Lowlands were quickly anglicised. Historically, the region has defended itself against oppressors.

IRON AGE

The Iron Age replaced the Bronze Age in about 500 BC with the arrival of the Celts who were skilled iron workers.

JACOBITES

These were supporters of James II. After he was overthrown in 1688, they received support from the Scots who were against the union of Scotland with England.

KURDS

The Kurds are a nomadic people who have been dispossessed of their land and now live in the area covering northern Iraq, eastern Turkey and western Iran.

LAW OF TANISTRY

This was an ancient system of alternate succession of rulers from two closely related families. It existed in Scotland until the eleventh century.

LOLLARD

A follower of John Wycliffe during the fourteenth, fifteenth and sixteenth centuries.

LONG BARROWS

Neolithic people buried their dead in long barrows, which are elogated mounds usually covering a burial chamber.

THE LOW COUNTRIES

Present-day Holland.

LOWLANDS

This is the flat region of central Scotland (see Highlands).

MEGALITHIC SETTLERS

Early settlers characterised by their construction of standing stones or 'megaliths'.

MESOLITHIC PERIOD

The Middle Stone Age has the first traceable inhabitants to Scotland. These hunters and fishermen inhabited the area from around 7000 BC.

MONOLITHS

A large block, obelisk or column of stone. Early settlers often erected them in concentric rings.

MORMAER

A governor.

NEOLITHIC PERIOD

The New Stone Age, 4000 to 2400 BC, saw the first permanent settlements made of wood and stone in Scotland.

REFORMATION

The Reformation of the Church in 1560 saw an end to many monastic communities and the foundation of the Church of Scotland and the Protestant Church in England.

ROYALISTS

The Royalists supported Charles I against Cromwell and his followers, known as the Roundheads. The Scots fought against the crown but were later manipulated by the King.

STONE CISTS

The Beaker people often interred their dead in these box-shaped burial chambers.

SUBSIDIARITY

In 1988, the Scottish National Party favoured a doctrine of subsidiarity, whereby small nations could preserve an independent identity within the larger framework of a united Europe.

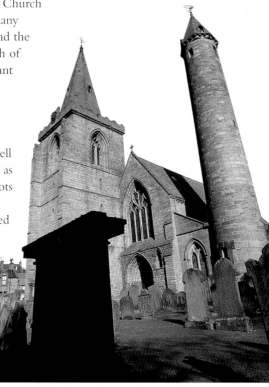

Recommended Reading

Barrow, Geoffrey W.S. *The Kingdom of the Scots* (1973)

Brand, J. *The National Movement in Scotland* (1978)

Brown, Jennifer *Scottish Society in the 15th Century* (1977)

Brown, P. Hume *History of Scotland* 3 vols. (1912)

Brown, Stewart J. and Fry, Michael *Scotland in the Age of the Disruption* (1993)

Burleigh, J.H.S. *A Church History of Scotland* (1962)

Cairncross, A.K. (ed) *The Scottish Economy* (1954)

Campbell, R.H. *Scotland Since 1707* (1966)

Chadwick, Nora *Celtic Britain* (1963)

Clarke, M.G. and Drucker, O.W. *Changing Scotland* (1976)

Clement, G.C. and Reid, G.L. *Scotland's Scientific Heritage* (1961)

Cowan, Ian B. *The Scottish Covenanters, 1660–1688* (1976)

Crawford, Barbara E. *Scotland in Dark Age Britain* (1995)

Cruden, Stewart *The Scottish Castle* (1963)

Cummins, W.A. *The Age of the Picts* (1995)

Devine, T.M. and Finlay, R.J. *Scotland in the 20th Century* (1996)

Dickinson, W. Croft *Scotland from the Earliest Times to 1603* (1977)

Donaldson, Gordon *Scotland, James V to James VII* (1974)

Donaldson, Gordon *The Scots Overseas* (1966)

Donaldson, Gordon *The Scottish Reformation* (1960)

Duncan, A.A.M. *Scotland: the Making of the Kingdom* (1975)

Edwards, Owen Dudley *A Claim of Right for Scotland* (1988)

Ellis, P.B. and Mac a'Gobhainn, S. *The Scottish Insurrection of 1820* (1970)

Fenton, Alexander *Scottish Country Life* (1976)

Ferguson, William *Scotland: 1689 to the Present* (1968)

Fleming, J.R. *The Church in Scotland* 2 vols (1927–33)

Gibb, Sir Alexander *Scottish Empire* (1937)

Glover, Janet *The Story of Scotland* (1960)

Gray, Malcolm *The Highland Economy* (1957)

Hamilton, H. *An Economic History of Scotland in the 18th Century* (1963)

Harvie, C. *Scotland and Nationalism* (1997)

Henderson, Isobel *The Picts* (1967)

Hunter, James *The Making of the Crofting Community* (1976)

Jones, G.H. *The Mainstream of Jacobitism* (1954)

Kermack, W.R. *The Scottish Highlands* (1957)

Kellas, James G. *Modern Scotland* (1980)

Lane, Jane *The Reign of King Covenant* (1956)

Lenman, Bruce *An Economic History of Modern Scotland* (1977)

Linklater, Eric *The Survival of Scotland* (1968)

Lynch, Michael *Scotland, a New History* (1996)

Lythe, S.G.E. and Butt, J. *An Economic History of Scotland, 1100–1939* (1975)

McCrone, G. *Scotland's Economic Progress, 1951–60* (1965)

Mackenzie, W. Mackay *The Scottish Burghs* (1948)

Mackie, J.D. *A History of Scotland* (1964)

Mackie, R.L. *A Short History of Scotland* (1962)

Maclean, Fitzroy *Scotland, A Concise History* (1970)

McWilliam, Colin *The Scottish Townscape* (1978)

Mathew, David *Scotland Under Charles I* (1955)

Menzies, G. *Who Are the Scots?* (1971)

Middlemas, R.K. *The Clydesiders* (1965)

Mitchison, Rosalind *A History of Scotland* (1970)

Nicholson, Ranald S. *Scotland: the Later Middle Ages* (1974)

Nicolson, N. *Lord of the Isles* (1960)

Petrie, Sir Charles *The Jacobite Movement* (1959)

Prebble, John *The Highland Clearances* (1963)

Prebble, John *The Lion in the North* (1971)

Pryde, George W. *The Treaty of Union 1707* (1950)

Rait, Sir Robert S. *The Parliaments of Scotland* (1924)

Ritchie, Graham and Anna *Scotland Archaeology and Early History* (1981)

Ritchie, R.L.G. *The Normans in Scotland* (1954)

Sadler, John *Scottish Battles* (1996)

Saunders, J.L. *Scottish Democracy 1815–1840* (1950)

Scott, Paul H. *Scotland, an Unwon Cause* (1997)

Smout, T.C. *A History of the Scottish People, 1560–1830* (1969)

Steel, Tom *Scotland's Story* (1984)

Stones, E.L.G. *Anglo-Scottish Relations, 1174–1328* (1965)

Tranter, Nigel *The Story of Scotland* (1987)

Wainwright, F.T. (ed) *The Problem of the Picts* (1955)

Webb, K. *The Growth of Nationalism in Scotland* (1977)

Webster, Bruce *Scotland from the 11th Century to 1603* (1975)

Wormald, Jenny (ed) *The New History of Scotland* 8 vols. (1984)

Author Biography

Dr James Mackay is a journalist and broadcaster, biographer and historian. A former saleroom correspondent of the *Financial Times*, he has also written numerous books on stamps, coins, antiques and other collectables. A history graduate of Glasgow University, he is regarded as the world's leading authority on Robert Burns.

Picture Credits

Index